MARGIN RELEASED

BOOKS BY J. B. PRIESTLEY
include the following:

COLLECTED PLAYS

Volume I

Dangerous Corner
Eden End
Time and the Conways
I Have Been Here Before
Johnson over Jordan
Music at Night
The Linden Tree

Volume II

Laburnum Grove
Bees on the Boat Deck
When We Are Married
Goodnight, Children
The Golden Fleece
How are they at Home?
Ever Since Paradise

Volume III

Cornelius
People at Sea
They Came to a City
Desert Highway
An Inspector Calls
Home is Tomorrow
Summer Day's Dream

Many other plays, full-length or one-act, can only be obtained in Acting
Editions published by Samuel French Ltd

NOVELS

Angel Pavement
The Good Companions
Faraway
They Walk in the City
Three Men in New Suits
Adam in Moonshine

Bright Day
Festival at Farbridge
Daylight on Saturday
Wonder Hero
The Magicians
Let the People Sing

TALES

Low Notes on a High Level
Saturn Over the Water
The Doomsday Men
Benighted

The Shapes of Sleep
The Thirty-First of June
Black-Out in Gretley
The Other Place (*short stories*)

ESSAYS AND AUTOBIOGRAPHY

Margin Released
Midnight on the Desert
English Journey

Thoughts in the Wilderness
Rain upon Godshill
Delight

Journey Down a Rainbow (*with Jacquetta Hawkes*)
All About Ourselves and Other Essays
(*chosen by Eric Gillett*)

CRITICISM

Literature and Western Man

The Art of the Dramatist
Meredith (*English Men of Letters*)

English Comic Characters
Peacock (*English Men of Letters*)

J. B. PRIESTLEY

MARGIN
RELEASED

A WRITER'S REMINISCENCES

AND REFLECTIONS

HARPER & ROW, PUBLISHERS

NEW YORK AND EVANSTON

Contents

Illustrations

Preface

This book is not an autobiography pretending not to be. Its subtitle describes it exactly—*A Writer's Reminiscences and Reflections*. Readers dipping into Parts One and Two might be forgiven for thinking they were looking at an autobiography; but they would be wrong. It is doubtful if dippers, as distinct from honest readers, are entitled to have any explanation from an author; nevertheless, for everybody's sake, I will explain how this book came to be written.

I wrote Part Three, *I Had the Time*, after a talk over lunch with Mr H. V. Hodson, then editor of the *Sunday Times*. We agreed I should write some literary reminiscences that could be serialised in the paper. From the first, however, I saw these thirty thousand words or so not as Sunday journalism but as part of a book, which I would have written even if the response to these *Sunday Times* instalments had not been so surprisingly favourable. (I had many friendly and even enthusiastic letters, after declaring that nobody wrote them any more, at least to me.) Passages cut or removed altogether from these instalments, to make room for photographs, have been restored in this text. I hope Mr Hodson, now at pasture in fresh fields, will accept my thanks.

It seemed to me then that this Part Three, covering forty years of my professional life, would be better understood if I described how I began writing, in the years before the First War, and then related, in a shorter Part Two, a kind of bridge section, what happened to me during that war. For choosing four extracts from these two Parts for publication in the *Sunday Times*, I must thank my friend Mr Leonard Russell. I must insist, however, that, no matter how far I may seem to wander from authorship in these chapters about my earlier life, I did not feel I was attempting an autobiography, I was still trying to write in the spirit of literary reminiscence and reflection.

A final remark about the title of this volume, which must puzzle those readers who, unlike me, have not spent years using typewriters. Almost all of these machines have a key labelled 'Margin Release', frequently needed by hasty and careless typists like myself. This is the explanation of *Margin Released*, though I hope it suggests more than the use of a typewriter key: something at least has escaped from that narrow frame which has a conceited reticence at one end and a diffident humility at the other, and has found release in these pages.

J.B.P.

PART ONE

The Swan Arcadian
(1910–1914)

1

More than half a century ago, living then in Toller Lane, Bradford, but all in another world, I was sixteen and I had to make a choice. I had to leave school that summer or I had to stay there to work for a university scholarship. No compromise was possible. There was not a chance of hanging on at school for a year or two, not doing very much. Neither the school nor my father, who had once taught there, would have tolerated it. You stayed on to begin some systematic hard slogging for a scholarship. Contrary to some reports, I have never been at any age a systematic hard slogger. I have seemed to myself at all times to be lacking in determination and self-discipline. If I have never been called indolent and irresolute, that is because hardly anybody knows anything. I have a reputation for energy and fertility, but chiefly among fellow writers who are neither energetic nor fertile, do not want to be, and probably dislike me anyhow. If I have written a great deal, this is largely because I have always had ideas for work to lure me on and on. Not all these ideas were good; many were indifferent, some terrible. But I have never been without them. They were just beginning to beckon then, about 1910; they are still beckoning now. One of them lured me into this chronicle beginning at the end of my schooldays, to which I must now return.

There was of course no certainty of my winning a scholarship to Oxford or Cambridge, but that did not worry me. Though lazy and quite incapable of applying myself to subjects that bored me, I had always done very well at school; I brought to the subjects I did like, such as English and History, a great deal that I discovered for myself outside school. In coming to a decision I was not influenced by any dread of failure; one thing I possessed, perhaps to the point of brashness, was self-confidence. No, the trouble was that even the prospect of success was not enticing. Nothing beckoned there. I didn't see myself in courts or quads, under dreaming spires; and nine years and a long war later, when finally I did arrive in Cambridge, I still didn't see myself there, never felt at home. Statutes about not playing marbles on the Senate House steps, that kind of thing, never made me giggle cosily; they merely irritated me. Unlike some of my school friends toiling not for a degree and a better job but already under the spell of tradition, that great English hocus-pocus, I felt even then alienated rather than attracted by everything that had been long established. I do not claim this lack of response to tradition as a virtue; in some respects it is a weakness, closing the mind to a whole range of feeling; though it does help one to examine the English social scene with detachment or a certain useful scepticism, especially when the traditional has become the bogus, power and money playing charades. Unbeckoned then, I decided to leave school.

One school friend, George, stayed on and won a scholarship to Cambridge. His father worked as a joiner in one of the big mills. His mother, a wiry little woman with excited black eyes and a curious hoarse voice, came from somewhere in the Midlands and brought with her an odd trick of speech, 'singing' becoming 'sin-Ging'. We did a lot of sin-Ging in their small front room on Saturday and Sunday nights. George and I both played the piano in the same slapdash style, but he had no voice and I had a loud one, not unsuitable for baritone ballads but happiest in noisy comic songs. He became my accompanist, both at home and elsewhere. Once I earned a guinea, with his assistance, at a Saturday night variety concert at the Mechanics Institute, where I forgot too many words and was not a success. This must have been particularly disappointing to the impresario – a seedy old pro, who billed me as *Jack Croly, of the leading London and Provincial Halls* – because he was a believer in phrenology and before engaging me insisted upon feeling my bumps; so that I must have been a phrenological disappointment too. George and I only hit the top of our form, I suspect, in that packed front room. Fortunately both his parents delighted in company and noise and family jokes, people coming and going, casual hospitality, the party spirit. I borrowed a few touches of his father for Jess Oakroyd in *The Good Companions*, but his mother, never downcast, always blazing-eyed, about six-and-a-half stone of indomitable femininity, was the greater character. And several months after George had left for Cambridge, after I had dutifully admired all the things he had to take with him, the flannels, the dinner jacket and the rest, I caught sight of her one very cold morning on my way to work. She was coming out of an office building, for once looking shrunken and fagged, after the cleaning she must have taken on to help pay for all those things so necessary in Cambridge. When George came home in the vacs we still made a lot of noise in the front room; now there were Cambridge jokes as well, about no-marbles-playing and eccentric dons and cap-and-gown exploits; good evenings still, but never to me quite the same. And later I arrived in Cambridge without flannels and dinner jacket, and rather grimly paid my way.

My life at school had been neither a joy nor a torment, mostly rather boring. It was not until years afterwards, when I listened with astonishment to men talking in clubs, that I realised how important schooldays were to the English. In the later Twenties, when I lived in Hampstead, I used to play a lot of lawn tennis, and between sets all the talk was of schools – 'Both our boys are at So-and-so – where is your boy going?' It seemed, and still seems, idiotic to me, all this school talk. But then of course I did not live at school; perhaps nobody should. Games I enjoyed, and even collected three medals, which vanished years ago. (But where do such indestructible things go?) Gymnastics I detested then and have never admired since; those Czech mass antics seem to me a horror, halfway to the anthill. Most of the hours spent in classrooms were tedious. I had a quick impatient mind and it fretted when some point had to be made over and over again. Later, in the Army, and much later still at conferences, I discovered the same reaction in myself, the same mixture of irritation and boredom. There was nothing wrong with the masters, but only one of them seemed to me to bring his subject, English, to life.

His name was Richard Pendlebury – a good name in my ears – and he died, long before he ought to have done, over forty years ago. He was tall, intensely dark, as handsome and commanding as an ideal Spanish grandee. His qualifications were modest, below our present standards; he had no Ph.D. for a thesis on the use of the semi-colon in the later works of George Eliot, but he loved good writing, and he knew how to communicate and share that love. Perhaps my feeling for literature could hardly be separated from my liking and admiration for Pendlebury himself. Probably I felt obscurely that the poems and plays and essays he read and discussed with us had helped to make him what he was, had given his glance a flash of fire, had brought a grave courtesy into his manner, had put glints of humour and a cutting edge into his talk. I can see and hear him again, quite clearly, across years that changed all human history; and if his influence on me was far greater, as indeed it was, than that of all the professors and lecturers I heard later in Cambridge and the critics I met in London, that was because I sat in a classroom, at the right time, with a teacher who loved good writing. But at school there would have been no more Pendlebury; I was already outside his orbit.

So I left school, tired of it. I wanted to write – though ready to conduct symphony orchestras and do a little great acting from time to time – and I believed that the world outside class-rooms and labs would help me to become a writer. Certificates and degrees, I felt, had nothing to do with authorship. More-over, not one of the living writers whose work excited me most had been to Oxford or Cambridge. No class feeling came into all this; I was neither a snob nor an anti-snob. This must seem strange now, when we are always reading – or at least are being asked to read – books and articles about the English class system. The truth is that in these early years I was barely conscious of its existence. When, about thirty years ago, Bernard Shaw came back from a visit to Russia, he told me it was a wonderful relief to be in a country that had no ladies and gentlemen. I said that I had spent the first twenty years of my life without meeting any of those ladies and gentlemen. This was true. I had been brought up in a West Riding industrial community, where to a youngster the social hierarchy was invisible. I am not pretending we had a miniature classless society there, but we probably came nearer to having one than anybody born in southern England can even imagine. Wool men who gambled and won generally left Bradford before they acquired a title and began entertaining the County. If they had come back, a lot of men wearing cloth caps and mufflers would still have called them Sam and Joe. It was not until I took a commission, later in the War, that I discovered that the class structure, with all its tangle of superiorities and in-feriorities, was not simply something useful to novelists and playwrights, almost like wills and wards and missing heirs, but something one might have to live with. I felt somewhat bewildered then, half-amused, half-indignant; and I think I have stayed like that ever since.

No, I simply wanted to have done with formal education. I was tired of people telling me things and then asking me how much I remembered. What I wanted was to look around and find things out myself, then try to write. Here, no doubt, I was pulling away from my father, as a lad of sixteen should do. My father was a schoolmaster, and I could never imagine him as anything else: teaching was his vocation. After teaching children all day he was ready to spend half his nights and nearly all his week-ends teaching adults. People he met in trains, country pubs, seaside boarding houses, found themselves being taught by him. He was no dictatorial and boring pedant; he was lively-minded and companionable, always eager to learn himself; but what he knew – and he knew a lot – he had to teach. He believed in Education as few people nowadays believe in anything. He and his father, a mill worker who probably earned about thirty shillings a week, together performed some little miracle of thrift so that he was able to go to a teachers' training college in London, some time in the Eighties; and there he found Education, a prize, a jewel, not a modern convenience laid on like hot and cold water. He belonged to a generation that believed we could educate ourselves out of muddle and wretchedness and black despair into the sunlight for ever. Its spokesman was H. G. Wells, one of my father's favourite authors, at least before *Ann Veronica* brought sex in, and sound Baptist chapel men, like my father, began shaking their heads. And of course it is true that Education can take us all from darkness into light, that is, so long as we are not thinking about actual schools, colleges, courses, examinations, degrees, but have in mind some rather vague dark-into-light process that may be called educational. Most of the demands for more and more education I have read these last few years do not suggest anybody is worrying about our civilisation, and the sort of minds at work on it, but only about competing for bigger or cheaper bombs and rockets, faster jets, cars that have telephones, and electric shoe-cleaners. Sometimes I think that every time the school makes one move up, the street outside, representing the environment that must win in the end, makes three moves down; as if all the children in a town were at last learning arithmetic but having their lessons in the local whore-house. Even before 1924, when he died, my father had lost some confidence. If he were alive now, he would be half out of his mind.

I was very fond of my father, indeed I loved him. He was unselfish, brave, honourable, public-spirited. He was the man socialists have in mind when they write about socialism. Bradford, after often hearing what he thought of it, came at last to cherish him; among the older citizens up there I have never really lived up to him, merely represent a showy falling-off. But he was not all of a piece; there were odd mixed elements in him. Though largely tolerant and humorous, there was a curious puritanical streak in him. One of our differences was that from childhood I was fascinated by any form of pro-fessional entertainment, whereas he was suspicious of it, considering it at best a waste of time and possibly a danger to sound character-building. Again, though not a pious type, he was one of the most conscientious and hard-working members of our Baptist chapel and its Sunday school, both of which I detested at all ages. He was also a fanatical sabbatarian, so that by the time I reached my teens and spotted the illogicalities he soon lost his temper in any argument we had about the Lord's Day. He had in fact an explosive temper, and with it a terrify-ing trick of suddenly breaking into violence, sweeping every-thing off a breakfast table, for example, or hurling an open suitcase down a flight of stairs. Any preparations for travel brought the flashpoint nearer, and the Priestley family often began its holidays in tears. But any storm soon passed; he was never sulky, silent, cold, sarcastic. He wanted to teach, to counsel, to guide, but not to gather and use power. Indeed, except during his occasional berserk moments, my father was a most lovable man.

Like so many good men – and unlike all the men I have known who have been corrupted in some way – my father was not afraid, at the right time and in the right place, to let go of his dignity and be a clown. He was never artfully funny; just downright frankly silly, like a boy among boys. He baulked at nothing in charades, which I helped to organise as soon as I was old enough to command any attention. In those days, before the wholesale and retail trades took over Christmas, there used to be parties every night or so, and many a time I laughed myself into a red haze and a danger of choking. (This may be happening now to small boys; perhaps I don't go to the right parties.) Until my middle teens, when I naturally wanted to go my own way and so had some sharp differences of opinion with my father, I was happy at home. My mother died not long after I was born, but I had a step-mother who defied tradition by always being kind, gentle, loving. Indeed, it was she who excused my teenage eccentricities, declaring, with that sardonic over-emphasis peculiar to women in the North, great flatterers of male pretensions, that I was a genius and therefore might be excused. (But you have to hear that 'geee-nius'.) Yes, I was happy there, so, wherever my desire to write came from, it certainly did not come out of any frustrated, wretched childhood. I was outside the fashionable literary movement before I even began. But at home I did hear too much about Education.

This was inevitable. Many of my father's friends were teachers too, belonging to the same generation of educational enthusiasts. Our house, where there was a great deal of that casual hospitality which largely vanished in the First War,

was noisy with the claims and protests of the teaching profession, all the noisier because these teachers, once they were
warm in argument, could not help using their classroom voices.
I lingered among their pipes and, in winter, toddy, for which
we had those silver sugar-crushers (and, remember, whisky
was three-and-sixpence a bottle then), hearing too much
about Education but enjoying the visitors as comic characters.
I think people who cannot appreciate such characters in
literature, finding them overdrawn, out of scale, larger and
simpler than life, must have lost all memory of their childhood
or had one that was unusually narrow and cheerless. When we
are very young, it is the friends of our parents, so enormously
themselves and so seemingly unchanging, like immortals, who
create for us our first comic characters. Later, when fiction and
drama present us with such characters, they take us back to a
time when all available rooms have been tidied and cleared and
the fires are burning bright, and we are anything between six
and twelve years old, giggling and scuffling in the background
while the great drolls arrive. It is useless to insist, as austere
and unimaginative criticism often does, that people are not
really like that, for there is a time when they are, and it is a
time that continues to exist out of reach of critical opinion, a
time we remember when we no longer recall which critic said
what. But though my father's friends did not fail me as comic
characters, nevertheless they talked too much about Education.
I was tired of it. I needed a change of atmosphere.

Now that I look back I am surprised that my father was not
violently angry nor even sadly reproachful when I told him I
wanted to leave school. (Or were there some scenes that
memory has blotted out?) I should like to think he had never
made a plan in which I went to a university. There may have
been in him a conflict between his bookishness, which later
accepted with pride anything of mine that got into print, and

his West Riding insistence upon livings being earned, corn being carried, and no monkey business and hanky-panky. I can understand now why my teenage antics should make him feel uneasy. His own family were mill workers, both men and women, but a solid steady sort; but he had plucked my mother, my real mother, about whom I know nothing except that she was high-spirited and witty, from the clogs and shawls 'back o't mill', a free and easy, rather raffish kind of working-class life, where in the grim little back-to-back houses they shouted and screamed, laughed and cried, and sent out a jug for more beer. He must have felt that it needed only a bit too much hanky-panky, just a few years trying this and that, with no corn to be carried, and down I would go, putting on a cloth cap and muffler to fetch another jugful of beer. Certainly something of the sort must have been at the back of his mind, for when I told him I wanted to leave school, without any immediate plan of earning a living, he announced that I must go into the Bradford trade, the wool business.

It was as if a fanatical teetotaller had told his son to get a job as a barman. My father himself would no more have gone into the wool trade than he would have joined the Foreign Legion. To him and his friends there was a composite and symbolic 'wool man' – and I can still hear them pronouncing the words with scorn – who was the enemy of teachers and the good life. There were of course some 'wool men' among my father's large acquaintance, but not one among his friends. He had, I suspect, a mental image of a 'wool man' that could have been used to represent capitalism in a socialist cartoon. A few of the richer dealers in raw wool, who had brought off some lucky gambles, were indeed fat and red-faced and loose-lipped and went off to the races behind enormous cigars. It was such men who infuriated my father and his friends by declaring that teachers were overpaid for what they did and had too many holidays. However, the wool trade, which began with bids in distant auction-rooms for the raw material and ended with the delivery of the dyed and finished cloth (and a sound Bradford man never accepted any cloth a tailor offered him, but picked his own suit length elsewhere) and so contained many different skills and levels of buying and selling, was Bradford's own trade, where there was solid brass among the muck. Any youth with a suspected weakness for hanky-panky might at last stand on his own two feet there. If he had 'anything about him' – a phrase I seem to remember – he could learn and then earn somewhere among the wool merchants, the combers, the spinners, the weavers, the dyers and finishers, the exporters; he could acquire a nice girl, a house of his own, a bedroom suite, a piano and a pram, with whist drives and chapel high-teas-and-concerts in the winter, and the summer rising to a peak in ten days at Scarborough or Morecambe. So into the wool trade I must go.

I agreed, partly to stop my father worrying, partly because I had no plan of my own. I knew that, in the Bradfordian sense, I hadn't anything about me: I was crammed with hanky-panky. I wanted to write but I had just enough sense to know that I must spend at least the next few years trying my hand at it. I also knew – and this was clever of me at sixteen – that work on a newspaper was no use to me, otherwise I would have rejected the wool trade and bluffed or wheedled myself into one of our three local dailies. I was already acquainted with several young reporters, whose sophistication seemed to me almost satanic; they could take the city to pieces over a coffee and roll-and-butter at Lyons's; they had even interviewed delectable beings appearing at the Theatre Royal or the Empire; they were already men of the world to my stammering oaf; but somehow I knew that what I wanted to do, whatever that might be, had to be kept clear of what they were doing. So for the time being it had to be the wool trade; any branch of it, for tops, noils, yarns, pieces, were all the same to me, I cared for none of these things. Letters were exchanged; I was seen and questioned and – probably because I didn't really care what happened – was given the job. I left school to become a very junior clerk with Helm and Company, Swan Arcade, Bradford.

2

I was not the office boy. Low as I was, there was one even lower. At times, however, we were between office boys, and then I had to fill ink-wells, put out blotting paper, uncover the typewriters, work the copying press, and take enormous bundles of samples to the General Post Office, a chore I particularly detested. But then I detested the whole sample side of the business; sometimes I felt my golden youth was slipping away between those sheets of blue wrapping paper. Now and again, it is true, the samples sent to us were not without a romantic interest. The muck that came out of the samples of camel hair brought eastern deserts into the office; on the sampling counter was dust from the road to Samarkand. Once I opened a parcel of Chinese pigtails, for millions of them had been cut off, following a state decree, and somebody in Shanghai was trying to tempt us into a new exotic branch of the trade. It was indeed a trade with odd little ramifications. I remember a firm that specialised in dolls' hair.

Our firm exported tops – wool that had been washed and combed and was ready to be spun into yarn – to spinners and manufacturers on the Continent. It bought raw wool, mostly at summer sales held in places like Andover, Marlborough, Devizes, sorted and blended it according to one formula or another, then sent it to the combing mills; and after much posting of samples to places all over Europe, and even as far as Rhode Island, we took such orders as came for these various tops of ours. Telephoning and writing to the transport companies, railway, canal, shipping, were among my duties, not entirely a dead loss, for in those free and easy years, before the law interfered with pleasant trade practices, I was able to sail to Copenhagen for exactly seven-and-sixpence, to Amsterdam for about half-a-crown. A man responsible for a business of this kind really had to know a good deal, not only about raw wool, tops, noils, yarn, but also about financial conditions in many different countries, which he would have to visit regularly, calling on his customers. But on the junior clerk level, from which I never rose, it was dull. There were always those cursed samples. There was also a thing called the bag-book that had to be kept up to date, though perhaps I should not grumble about that because I was able to read volume after volume of poetry, hidden in my desk drawer, while pretending to be busy with this bag-book. Letters not only in English but also in French and German had to be typed, then copied, not by using carbons or some duplicating machine but by inserting them between the dampened sheets of a copying book, which was then squeezed in a big heavy press. We had no girl typists to make tea, to give us bright glances, to introduce into this male routine the disturbing feminine principle. Ours was an entirely masculine office, without a touch of feminine grace and light, everything there solemn and weighing tons. A girl or two might have made a wonderful difference. To this day I am suspicious of all social functions that are entirely male, clubs and stag parties and pompous banquets with never a woman in sight.

I had to be there at nine sharp, had an hour for lunch, but no time when I could say I had done enough and could go home.

Occasionally we finished at six, more often about six-thirty, and sometimes after seven, when we were given sixpence for 'tea money'. Whatever the hour was, before leaving we had to go into the boss's private office and ask if there was anything more. Here we were out of luck. Most wool firms were bossed by men who had wives and children to return to, who on light evenings wanted an hour or two in the garden or a round of golf, who hurried away in winter for a drink and a rubber of bridge. We had to ask permission to leave the office from the one man whose business was most of his life, who was capable of spending Christmas Day or Good Friday brooding over samples and ledgers, who could not understand how we could tear ourselves from exporting tops. So when we asked him if there was anything more – and I soon acquired a manner and tone of asking that ought to have made anything but a negative reply very difficult – all too often there *was* something more. He may have thought he was doing us a favour, offering a last-minute rescue from the empty hours outside, but even he must have guessed that he had no hope of converting me, that every day my real life began about the time his ended. Why I wasn't sacked after the first few months, I couldn't imagine then. It must have been obvious that I did not take the business seriously. I was lazy and careless; I wore what were by Bradford trade standards outlandish clothes; the time I took on any errand outside the office was monstrous, a scandal. True, I was paid very little, but even on that low rate I was bad value. Why then was I allowed to stay, never sacked, in the end taking myself off to join the Army in the late summer of 1914?

I can only think now that somehow I must have represented a part of himself that this austere elderly man had repressed but not altogether destroyed, an idle, smoking, drinking, girl-chasing, verse-writing, floppy-tie-wearing self buried but still

not lifeless under a mountain of wools, tops, and noils. Somewhere behind that formidable persona – and he was one of the
very few men of whom I have felt afraid – was a secret sym-
pathiser, a small anti-business fifth column. He was unlike
most wool men not only in his austere style of life – for the only
vice he allowed himself to enjoy was a muttered cursing when
an order had been missed or the wrong samples had been sent –
but also because he was well-read. And I was often sent to a
superior lending library to find a good new book for him. This
was only five minutes away, but he ought to have known –
certainly the cashier could have told him – that I would be out
of the office for the better part of an hour, enjoying my pipe –
we were not allowed to smoke at work – and observing the
town through an almost stupefying haze of Cut Black
Cavendish, 3½d an ounce at Salmon and Gluckstein's. I had
no personal relationship with him, never exchanging any
friendly words from first to last; his second-in-command,
responsible for the office work, rather disliked me, knowing I
was idle and rebellious; I had no good looks, no charm, to set
off against my failings; so it must have been some buried self
of his that kept me from the sack, some vague unspoken
sympathy with my literary aspirations. There may have
been a time, round about 1875, when he thought about
turning author. If not, then this is a mystery without a single
clue.

One end of the office, with a broad counter, served as a
sampling room; we did our clerking at the other end, which
had high desks and tall narrow stools and a Dickensian air. But
it lacked both the cosy comedy and the menace of Dickens, and
was in fact dull. I much preferred the atmosphere of the firm's
warehouse, where the wool arrived to be sorted. This was
about half a mile away, not too close to Market Street and the
centre of the city, on the near edge of a whole region of ware-

houses and mills. I was always having to go up there, and was very friendly with the permanent warehouseman, whose name, I am sorry to say, I have forgotten, though I can recall his face and voice without hesitation, and remember his essentially Bradfordian manner, a mixture of grumbling, irony, dry wit. He was paid thirty shillings a week and was bringing up a family on them; and, while life must have been spare and rough, I don't think any of his daughters were going off with lorry-drivers or his sons were amusing themselves kicking somebody to death. The wool-sorters, who came and went and were not on wages but on piece-work, were a change from my anxious fellow clerks, for they were skilled men, who didn't give a damn, preferring to regular hours and wages a week or so of hard work followed by a few days' lolling and boozing. (This irregular rhythm of effort and relaxation, I believe, is what most of us English really like; we are not happy as a people with the machine tempo of modern industrialism, often going on strike to prove we are not yet robots.) The possession and application of a skill – and the speed with which they sifted and disposed of the wool was astonishing – gave these wool-sorters a stiffening of self-respect not many clerks have ever had. They knew they were men and so behaved like men; this inner dignity allowed them to dispense with any outward show of it. As I went almost sliding along the greasy floor of the warehouse, dodging between the bales, I would be greeted by the sorters, caps on the backs of their heads, pipes in their mouths; and one of them might roar, 'Na, lad! Ah see tha's gotten that daft bloody coat on again.' Nobody talked like that in the office, where that same coat – it was a dashing and voluminous sports jacket in a light chrome green – had met stares and murmurs of disapproval. I would have been happier, I think, working in the warehouse.

Swan Arcade, where we had our office, several floors up, had entrances in three different streets – and very high imposing entrances they were too – but the main approach, which happened to be the one nearest to my tram, was from Market Street. I thought it a fine street during those years, and now, looking back, I do not believe youth and inexperience were deceiving me. Unlike the other streets in the centre of the town, it was not too narrow and it was level. Unlike them too, it had a metropolitan look, an air of massive opulence; it was a thoroughfare fit for men who would, as they said, 'cut up for a pretty penny'. Now that it has been tastelessly improved, it has lost all character; but in those days its solid buildings of smoke-blackened stone, unbroken by façades that looked bright for a month and then a dingy mistake ever afterwards, pleased the eye. I cannot believe that the people who see nothing in West Riding towns but unrelieved ugliness really use their eyes. They are not looking as a painter would look; they are at the mercy of an idea of Victorian industrialism; here are large square buildings, not old, not quaint, and here is stone that the smoke and grime of industry has darkened, therefore the total effect must be ugly. And it may be nothing of the kind; indeed, at times it can seem beautiful.

Day after day I hurried along Market Street towards Swan Arcade and the office, often aware of exquisite compositions of light and shadow, of smoke and sunlight and dark stone. In summer and early autumn especially, there would be great dramatic shafts of sunlight together with brown misty openings, dividing and subtly illuminating the blackened façades. At the far end, as I went towards the office, where the glass-roofed Midland Station completed the square into which the street opened, there was often a brightness, a bewildering dazzle, that was a promise of adventure and ultimate triumph. And nose joined eye in appreciating the prospect. True, there were places not far away that stank and were abominable. To go along Canal Road on a warm day, as I often had to do, passing between a sulphuric acid works and a hide-and-skin establishment (is there a worse reek?) was to know an olfactory ordeal. But there was a centre-of-Bradford smell, there in Market Street too except when the rains were washing it away, characteristic and unmistakable, and not acrid, not unpleasant, though there was smoke and a touch of soot in it that my nose is glad to remember. Often since then, when I have found myself in some particularly cavernous large railway station, its tawny-to-indigo gloom and smoky sunlight and smell have returned me to mornings in early June and September when I hurried along Market Street, late for the office.

Except for a tobacconist's, where I sometimes bought an ounce or two, tempted by the display of navy cuts and plugs a foot thick, the shops along Market Street, few but choice, and its bars and grill-rooms were not for me. Just before I dodged into the Arcade itself I had to pass every day the windows of a very grand men's outfitters, so sure of itself that it disdained any mention of price; and I doubt if it ever occurred to me that what I saw in those windows could be at any time within my reach. Although I was then going through a dandy phase, trying to be dressy – in a floppy-tie and pegtop-trousers style – on tuppence, I believe I only admired what I saw, gave none of it a hungry stare. In spite of my largely frustrated dandyism, I felt little or no envy of anybody. I remember states of mind far better than I do actual events, and I think I am not deceiving myself when I declare that then and later I was rarely troubled by envy. I am not, never have been, an envious man. It is not other men's good fortune but some disappointing feature of my own that starts me grumbling. Secretly I expect too much. 'Is that all?' I cry to myself. But in all this there is no envy, certainly none of that terrible envy of other people's happiness which stains and corrupts life.

What I often did feel then was something very different, which I tried to express over thirty years later in a novel called *Bright Day*. It was a sense of some mysterious and magical life being led by families or groups, into which I longed, wistfully rather than enviously, to find my way. It took me years and years to learn that it is the mystery that creates the magic, that the enchantments imagined on the outside vanish almost immediately once you are inside, that indeed what is truly magical rises from your own depths. (Of all these illusions Proust is the master analyst.) There are many parts of the world, far too many, where a square meal is a marvel; to people who have nothing a little of anything can seem a shining bonus; but when we have reached the level of living most of us know in the West, we should tell ourselves, defying the advertisers, that nobody is having the wonderful time we are encouraged to imagine. Even to those smiling couples for ever being served cocktails and canapés by air hostesses, life is just going on. We change its quality from within ourselves, not by going somewhere and buying something. But now we spend billions encouraging illusions and stoking up envy, and most of them would be better spent providing a square meal and a whole shirt on some other continent where want is real and needs no advertisement. Perhaps the only advertisement that ever really fascinated me was one I saw during these Swan Arcade years; it was in a newspaper, quite small, plainly worded, without any suggestion of glamour, and it was for a forester. Do not ask me now why I thought then I could be happy as a forester – perhaps I had recently been listening to somebody, Elena Gerhardt probably, singing German *Lieder* – but I answered that advertisement. Their answer was plainly worded too and still without glamour: they did not want me.

There was to be no escape from Swan Arcade through the forest.

This does not mean I disliked Swan Arcade itself. To begin with, I am an arcade man, and suspect that only some unsleeping evil principle, for ever at work among us English, prevents our having more of them. Moreover, Swan Arcade was no ordinary roofed-over huddle of gift shops; it was on the grand scale. (I prefer the past tense because even now machines, secretly directed by that evil principle, may be clawing it down to spread the glass-and-concrete monotony from Brasilia to Bradford.) When it was opened in 1879, it was saluted as 'the most complete building of its kind in Yorkshire, if not in England'. But this description, doing it the barest justice, does not deserve to be called a salute. Angus Holden, who built it, was one of Bradford's mayors and prominent in the local trade, but in him every spark of imagination had not been smothered by bales of wool; if he had not actually been to Milan or Genoa, then he had peered for hours at a stereoscope, very popular in the Seventies, or had been visited by odd dreams; and though his investment must have been profitable, as it deserved to be, somehow he or his architect or his builder contrived to give the place an air of not being strictly commercial, even a suggestion of a splendid folly. I am not thinking about the name now, for the Swan comes from a coaching inn, one of the old buildings that had to be pulled down to make way for the grand new arcade.

Among English arcades it was a giant, five storeys high. The skylights were so far above my head that I hardly ever gave them a glance. I seem to remember up there an airy clutter and complication of galleries, windows, straight and curved metal supports and struts. At each corner were stairs and lifts going up to various office floors, premises like ours; between these corners, inside the building, were smaller blocks of offices and what the trade called 'market-rooms'; and along the ground-floor aisles, beneath the forgotten skylights, which were of a sort to keep the interior darkish, were no ordinary shops (the original and highly sensible intention was to have them there, and of course there was opposition) but rather gloomy agencies and establishments, the kind that had brown wire screens in the windows to dishearten common people. There must have been a shop or two, though, gentlemanly and aloof, for I remember I used to visit one of them, a tailor's, filled with rolls of the gravest worsted, the darkest serge, the blackest broadcloth for prospective mourners. There I went to chat with the tailor himself, an acquaintance of mine who had a passion for amateur theatricals and the more dignified, though unsympathetic, roles in Galsworthy's *Silver Box* and various Manchester repertory plays.

As soon as you were carried up by the lift, you were walled in by the Bradford trade and the price of Crossbreds. But between the street outside and the approach to the lift, passing through the arcade, you were not in Bradford at all, just for a minute. You darted out of Market Street into the shade through one of the unnecessarily magnificent entrances; you moved along the marble floor in the hushed interior, with its hint of assignations among colonnades; you hurried past the mysterious screened windows of those unimaginable agencies and establishments down every aisle. Then you felt for a moment, just before the cage of the lift closed, you had been in some alien but not unfriendly city, a thousand miles from the West Riding, and that if you made a dash for the nearest exit you might find yourself in a street belonging to an altogether different kind of life. Swan Arcade, I think, helped to keep me hopeful. An inefficient and bored junior clerk I might be; indeed, I was; but I was also, you might say, a Swan Arcadian.

3

Not long after I had arrived at the office in the morning and had put on the chequered overall known locally as a 'brat', I would be pecking away at one of the two typewriters, which lived in a space between our high desks and the long sampling counter. They were enormous machines, giant primitives, hard to lift. They had no shift device; every letter, small or capital, every sign, had its separate key; and as we needed various accents for our foreign correspondence as well as fractions and the like for invoices, the keyboard looked like that of an organ. Moreover, they were built like battleships, solid metal, none of your tinny stuff. Six of the portables I use now would not have made one of them. If touch-typing were possible, I cannot imagine how, on such keyboards, where I had always to go searching for the next letter or sign. To this day, after working on typewriters for over forty years, ever since I became a professional writer, I use only my two fore-fingers, still pecking if no longer hunting. But touch-typing is meant for copyists; we others peck our way into creation, helped rather than hindered, I have come to believe, by what our fingers have to do. And there is a cold objectivity about the typewritten page that is good for an author. A man does not fall in love with his typing as men can do with their pretty handwriting or as men who dictate do with the sound of their own voices. Unlike the pen, the typewriter makes no attempt to excuse your faults; its page comes closest to the print at which all authors are aiming. I have never regretted reducing the pen to a scrawler of notes and signatures; and when, my fingers stiffer than such last thoughts as I may have, I can no longer type, then I will forswear authorship for ever.

It was years later, however, when I had left Swan Arcade and the First War had come and gone, that I owned a typewriter of my own. I think I typed out some verses now and again on one of the office machines, probably between one and two o'clock, when my seniors were out at lunch and I had returned from mine. No copying that took more time would have been possible. Even during this hour telegrams and cables came over the telephone, often elaborate and in German, making me curse and sweat as I pressed the round earpiece harder and harder with my left hand and fumbled and scrawled with my right. And now I am wondering how I contrived to send to editors so many typewritten stories and articles. The few that remain were certainly not copied on our office machines. They are in various types, all different from ours. I must have persuaded several girls I knew, real typists, to make copies for me, though, with one exception, I cannot recall how and when they were able to do this or how they were able to read my original script, nearly always written closely in pencil and smudgy. The exception, however, I do remember.

She had her own typing agency near our office, across a side-street. I was more than half in love with her for a year or so, and the fact that she was older than I was did nothing to diminish her attraction. If at times I was jealous of fully adult males taking her somewhere with more money to spend in two hours than I had to last me a week, there were other times when I knew I was cutting them out, talk defeating their swagger and prodigality – their five-shilling stall against my sixpenny gallery. Memories distant in time, unlike recent memories, begin to reveal themselves if we search for them. Into what I thought was a blank has come a clear image of this particular girl, a saucy dark lass, like the woman Shakespeare seems to have loved and then hated, with raven curls, bold eyes, a white skin. Rainy summer evenings return – I can almost catch the long lost smell of the rain-pitted dust on the roads – and under the floppy tweed hat that girls wore then on such evenings a few curls escape, to glitter with raindrops, and I see again the curved pale cheek, the pouting of the dark full lips, the fields and woods that vanished years ago, the dusty roads that are now motor highways, crowded with people wondering where to go. Now I remember she would keep her basement office open after business hours not only for kisses but sometimes for copying, my copying. She could only have been paid in kisses, for I had no money, but that does not mean I was being calculating and cold-blooded, for there had been a lot of kisses long before she saw the first of my difficult pencil scripts. It surprises me now she should have worked overtime and for nothing for someone as young and oafish as I was; but like many another saucy girl she was probably soft-hearted.

The writing itself was done at home, where I had transformed the front attic, my bedroom for years, into a sitting-room of sorts. A small gas-fire had been installed up there, but, apart from that, everything that had to be done I had to do myself. We were not poor and lived comfortably, but there was no money to spare, certainly not for any fancies of mine. On the colour-washed walls I pinned reproductions of pictures I liked. I cut and trimmed and then stained some orange boxes, which really looked like bookcases, at least in artificial light. Many of the books in them I had been able to buy only by spending tuppence instead of the eightpence I was allowed for lunch. I soon acquired an expert knowledge of how far tuppence would go not in satisfying but in blunting the appetite: there was, for example, one shop in the covered market that sold off stale buns that could at least be eaten if not enjoyed, and another shop, specialising in health foods, had a line in slabs of mashed dates and cocoanut which, when washed down with plenty of water in the chained iron cups of public drinking fountains, murdered appetite, so to speak, with a blunt instrument. Most of the books I was able to buy were chosen from those lists of the World's Best that deceive innocent youth, so that I was never able to finish reading some of them then and have never read them since. Others, wiser purchases, mostly of standard poets, still have a place on my shelves and a larger place in my affections. Between the bed and the gas-fire, a fierce little thing that could not begin to warm the room without grilling your shins, there was just enough space for two smallish old armchairs, so that when I was not scribbling and scribbling away I could entertain a friend – male of course, no girls allowed up there.

I was immensely proud of this room of mine, though temperamentally, as I soon discovered later, I am not the possessive house-proud type. It was my own place. Once I had climbed those stairs and closed the door behind me, to find myself under that sloping roof, I was no longer a junior wool clerk. I was a writer – poet, story-teller, humorist, commentator and social philosopher, at least in my own estimation. Even the editorial rejection slips, which arrived regularly, had value up there, proof that it was the literary life, not the wool trade, that was being lived behind that dormer window. I did not go as far as a youth I knew, also in the wool trade and a literary aspirant, who papered a cottage with rejection slips. I do not remember cherishing them in this fashion. Besides, I did come to have a few things accepted and printed, which he never did. But they helped to give my attic its character. All day, as I wrapped and unwrapped those damnable samples and wrote out little tickets for the stuff we were offering f.o.b. Gothenburg or Hamburg, I was conscious of the fact that it was waiting for me, a refuge, a stronghold among barbarians, an entrance into the larger life.

There are moments when I wonder if time has been shrinking, not just for me but for our whole world. They arrive when I remember what we youngsters were able to cram into those years before 1914, the last so many were to know. Now I cannot imagine how we found time for all we did. Some of my closest friends, rather older than I was, I must confess had easier or at least more regular hours of work than I had : one was an uncertificated teacher (he kept himself entirely, joining in everything, on nineteen shillings a week), one worked in a bank, another was a railway clerk. But consider me. The office claimed me from Monday to Friday until any time between six and seven, and it might be later; and I was there every Saturday morning until about half-past one. (A young man wrote to me, not long ago, saying in effect that it was all very well for me to air my views, but I didn't know what it was like to work in an office five days a week from nine to five. He was right; I never did.) Then, in the hours that were left, there was all the writing, to which I shall return. But this was only the beginning. Bradford then had two theatres and two music-halls, all under our patronage. I was especially fond of the fourpenny balcony at the Empire – not the cheapest seats, for there was a tuppenny gallery behind us – where I forgot my discomfort – the expert 'packers' treated us like sardines – looking down on Grock and Little Tich and W. C. Fields and Jimmy Learmouth, a comedian unknown to London, perhaps because he died young, who still seems to me the funniest man I have ever seen on the stage. Ours was a musical town : the Hallé came regularly, and Nikisch brought the London Symphony; there were many chamber concerts, and once for ninepence I heard trios by Kreisler (then at his best), Casals and Bauer; we had our own symphony orchestra, sketchy and with the most undependable horns that can ever have been heard in public, but not to be despised in those pre-recording days; and I hardly ever missed a concert of any importance. It was the era of Ysaye and Kubelik, Pachmann and Rachmaninov and Busoni, men who appeared to have more dominating and warmer personalities than the technical perfectionists who came later. The War did something to music too; afterwards there were too many graves, too much cruelty and folly to be remembered, for the old zest and warmth.

Then we had an Arts Club and a Playgoers' Society, which read, making quite a performance of it, the plays not likely to find their way to the Theatre Royal. We argued for hours and hours in pubs and cafés and on long walks, usually over the moors. On the edge of the moors, some of our friends rented cottages at ninepence a week, and gave us beds of a sort if we talked too late for the tram service down below. We were always falling more or less in love, and girls then were coy, elusive, time-consuming creatures, not meeting the predatory young male halfway as they seem to do now. (Sometimes I suspect that men of my generation, condemning the sexual looseness of this age, have never examined their minds to discover any envy lurking there.) In summer there were holidays and week-ends spent walking or staying in somebody's moorland cottage; and in winter, especially around Christmas, there were family and other parties, always late in the evening of course, no cocktail nonsense. On top of all this my friends and I read widely, both new books and old, and had a look somewhere at most of the weeklies, more numerous then than now. With far less time of our own than youngsters have now, how did we do all this? I don't know. Perhaps the very hours began shrinking during the murderous imbecility of the First World War. I will swear that afternoons were never the same again, shrinking to a pallid characterless interval between lunch and tea : all the great golden afternoons, when a man might plan an epic and even begin it, came to an end in August 1914.

Something else came to an end too – or so it seems to me, recalling my own experience. After the War I could not have remained in or near Bradford, never considered doing so. Before it I had no plans, not even daydreams, for leaving the West Riding for London. I was of course much younger then, still in my teens, but this does not altogether explain why I never even thought about London, except as a collection of editors' addresses. I was not too young to have hopes of leaving home, closing the office door for the last time, and finding a cottage somewhere not far from the moors, only a tuppenny tram-ride from the centre of the town and then a sharp walk, there to earn my living by writing. If I could have averaged a pound a week, I would have gone. This was my plan, my hope, my daydream; London, except as a buyer and provider, never came into it. I never imagined myself living more than ten miles away. And this does not mean that I was a stay-at-home, for before the War I had already been as far as Denmark, Sweden, Holland, Belgium, Germany. No splendid fortune, no sumptuous styles of life, came into such day-dreams as I had. A pound a week and a cottage were all I asked.

What came to an end during the First War – at least in my experience – was a kind of regional self-sufficiency, not defying London but genuinely indifferent to it. My father, for example, never read a London newspaper. What happened 'down South', outside politics, was no concern of his. It would never have occurred to him or his friends that people living in London might be envied. Certainly there has been plenty of complacent provincialism during these last forty years. Before the War, however, we were not even thinking of ourselves as being provincial; we were not adopting an attitude towards London, being obstinate about staying where we were; we enjoyed an innocent self-sufficiency, people at home where they belonged. London was to me simply a place to which most manuscripts had to be sent. Bradford seemed to offer me all I wanted from a town, and already I had a deep affection for the surrounding countryside that I have not lost in half a century. The office and its trade imprisoned me, but not the town, not the region, where I felt free and in my own place. Had I been born ten years later, I think I could never have felt like this; as soon as I had started writing, the idea of London would have tugged at me.

Now those were the years – say, 1911 to 1914 – that set their stamp upon me. Even if I had wanted to destroy their effect – and I never did – I could never really have succeeded. Now that I am remembering what I felt then, I begin to understand something that has often puzzled me. Many people, with publishers, editors, radio and television producers among them, assume even now that either I have never left the North or arrived the day before yesterday on the express from Leeds, whereas in fact I have lived in or near London for close on forty years. I seem to exist in a little atmosphere, all my own, of rather naïve provincialism, repelling the interest and admiration of the smart, the sophisticated, although I am not, never have been, a regional writer, and have travelled more and further than all but a very few English authors of our time. Appearance? Certainly, faces like mine, glowering puddings, can be seen in any backstreet between Sheffield and Skipton. Manner? I doubt it. Voice? Well, I still try to keep my vowels open, but – mimics, please note – I do not in fact use, except when clowning, the standard West Riding style of speech, which is both flatter and rather more nasal than mine. No, this suggestion of a naïve provincialism comes from those distant years that set their stamp upon me. I belong at heart to the pre-1914 North

Country. Part of me is still in Bradford, can never leave it, though when I return there now I wander about half-lost, a melancholy stranger. I am in the right place but not at the right time. But in the world outside, as I move from Stockholm to Montreal, Tokio to Santiago, Chile, something at the core of me is still in Market Street hearing the Town Hall chimes.

At that time I was surrounded by people who read a great deal, cared a lot for at least one of the arts, and preferred real talk and, if necessary, loud hot argument to social chit-chat. (The same kind of people, the same background and atmosphere, are described with loving precision by Neville Cardus in his autobiography.) But there were no professional writers among them, not an author in sight. Somewhere in London there was Oliver Onions, a Bradford writer with an odd history. Some eerie short stories, *Widdershins,* and some solid novels, *Good Boy Seldom, In Accordance with the Evidence, The Debit Account, The Story of Louie,* brought him a reputation that began to fade, like so many other things, during the First War. Then, after the Second War, he began all over again in his seventies, writing mediæval tales not at all like lending-library historical fiction, capturing readers who had never heard of him as one of the sociological novelists of the pre-1914 decade. Between the wars in London I sometimes met his wife, Berta Ruck, who wrote serials for girls' papers but did not identify herself with them; Onions himself I never did meet, and I am sorry, for he was a man of talent and an original. However, I did exchange a few words with a story-teller who had a large admiring public at that time and actually lived in Bradford. This was Cutcliffe Hyne, a huge fellow without any literary pretensions, a sportsman rather than an author, who created Captain Kettle, a character I refused to believe in after the age of fourteen. In his earlier years Hyne had roamed the world, then larger and more mysterious than it is now, and he really did know the remote and exotic backgrounds of his tales, but he kept Kettle too long on the boil. Even at seventeen, anxious to write my way out of a wool office, I never wanted to be another Cutcliffe Hyne. And, anyhow, I wasn't a sportsman.

Somewhere in this room, where I am writing among too many books that have never been put in any sensible order – I am too lazy to do it myself and too modest to demand professional help – there is a small fifty-year-old volume: *Ioläus and Other Poems* by James A. Mackereth. It was the first book ever given to me by its author. Indeed, Mackereth was the first published author, a real author with a row of volumes and press-cuttings and copies of angry or grateful letters to literary editors and reviewers, with whom I formed a friendship. And not only was he a poet but he looked like my idea of one. Nobody could have mistaken him for a wool merchant. He wore the roughest tweeds, shaggier than anything we see now, thick boots, a rather high-crowned soft hat; and his face followed one of Nature's fashions already then on the wane, for it was long, beak-nosed, hollow-cheeked, with eyes deep-set under a broad low forehead, the kind of face most tragedians of the later nineteenth century seemed to have. If all this suggests charlatanry, I am doing badly; he was a sound human being and a true, if not distinguished, poet. He had come from the Lake Country to work in a Bradford bank, and then after some years either he or his wife inherited sufficient money to keep a small family in decent comfort, probably less than it costs now to keep a motor car; so he quitted the bank for ever and divided his days between writing poetry and working in his garden. Perhaps he might have been a better poet – and he was not a bad one, and up to 1914 was well reviewed and appeared in some of the best weeklies – if he had not turned his back so completely on the bank, had taken a little of it with him, remembering as he sang with the larks on the moors what he had known in Market Street and Kirkgate. He was, you might say, too determinedly poetical, too *gladsome* and *elfin* in one mood, too *weird* and *eldritch* in another, too exuberantly romantic in a fashion already going out, so that men with smaller and shabbier gifts of heart and mind soon received more attention and respect than he did. The luck, which only genius, not talent, can ignore, was against him; and very bravely he pretended, especially to a youngster like me, not to care. But even then I knew he did; though he never knew I knew he did; I looked another way when some bitter creature seemed to be eating the roses.

Yeats apart, my friend Mackereth was *more like a poet* than any other I have seen and heard. He took a poetical view of everything, manfully defending it too, and men like my father, who did not want to read poetry at all out of school hours, regarded him with respect. The fact that I was on constant visiting terms with him – and of course he was much older than I was – encouraged my father to take my literary aspirations rather more seriously. The poet lived in a snug low-built house about three or four miles away, out in the country, well beyond trams and street-lamps and electricity; and during those years I must have walked scores of leagues, there and back, calling on him, generally uninvited. (We curse the telephone too easily.) When I was young, indeed until I got married and lived with the feminine social conscience, it never crossed my mind that any visit I paid anybody might be inconvenient, perhaps downright unwelcome. I assumed that the talk that had kept us up late on Tuesday was the passport to an unannounced visit on Friday. This was not conceit, only the large innocence of youth, believing the world to be simpler and better than it is.

On summer evenings I would talk with Mackereth in his

garden until all was a green dusk, then we would retire to his study and light the lamps. Tea and slices of cake would be brought in by his wife, a composed handsome lady with whom I was never at ease, suspecting she disliked me – as well she might, I see now. Then he and I would light our pipes and she would leave us, to go to bed, and he would read something he had just written, using that deep chanting tone which still seems to me better than any other for verse that has any lyrical flow. About midnight I would stride out for home, meeting nobody on the road. There were few cars about then – I rarely saw one on that road at night – but occasionally I would see a belated great waggon: most of them went earlier, keeping together like the covered waggons that opened the American West and creaking across the Pennines to Lancashire. Low in the sky over on my left were what might appear to be unfamiliar constellations; they were the street-lamps on the slopes of the hills opposite, above the invisible valley where the mills and the town began. The late hour and the walk, together with what so much talk and tobacco, perhaps tea and cake, had done to me, opened my mind then to that sense of un-limited possibilities, both in this life and some other, which has been described so often by the romantics. The poet's company and then the sharp walking under the stars lifted me into

> that blessed mood,
> In which the burthen of the mystery,
> In which the heavy and the weary weight
> Of all this unintelligible world
> Is lightened.

I was then a fairly commonplace lad, I think, not very different from a few hundred thousand of my contemporaries, so many of them soon to die, caught in barbed wire entanglements, obliterated by shellfire, suffocated by Flanders mud. I was luckier than most, having found a poet, ampler and finer in his talk perhaps than in his writing, to receive me in his garden and take me into his lamplit study. There, certain not ignoble expectations, which youth brings with it to the common scene, knew some degree of satisfaction, fulfilment. I believe such expectations, a feeling that life should have warmth, generosity, nobility, arrive with each generation; they are not taught but somehow inherited. When they are derided and frustrated, then contempt and bitterness and anger take their place. When the young behave badly, as we are told so many of them do now, it is because society has already behaved worse. We have the teenagers, like the politicians and the wars, that we deserve.

4

It is a great pity, I realise now, that I have never been a methodical man, carefully preserving what ought to be kept. I have gone marching on, probably towards the sea of oblivion, like Sherman through Georgia, burning and destroying as I went. Apart from some letters, a few pages of notes, an original script here and there, hardly anything has survived. There are no volumes of press-cuttings, no collections of programmes and photographs of the innumerable play productions; and any critical biographer who could survive my own discouragement – and several have already failed to – would find himself soon more profoundly discouraged by the lack of material. There is in front of me now, as I write, a mottled box-file, ragged at the edges, and I do not know how and when it arrived. What I do know is that it is a piece of luck I never deserved, for it contains not only many of the letters I

wrote home from the First War but also some assorted
samples of the stuff I was writing up in that attic, fifty years
ago. Nothing in print is here, none of the rare triumphs; and
what became of them – for one of us at home must have cut
them out and cherished them – I cannot imagine. They can be
tracked down of course; everything in public print in this
century is filed away somewhere. Indeed, I have an alarmingly
zealous bibliographer, who has already found some of them
and has offered me guidance. But the only research I want to do
here is into the recesses of memory, where laziness helps and
brisk visits to libraries would only hinder; so these surviving
specimens, fortunately various, must serve.

Opening the box-file, I have to get past the First War, as
memory itself has to do, for here on top are the old green
Active Service envelopes, bundled in white tape. With them
are a few other things out of that war: what is left of a red
leather wallet containing a faded photograph of the family, a
regimental shoulder-badge, not in metal but khaki cloth, and
the fragile remains of one of the old ten-shilling notes, which
looks as if it had been half-eaten by a rat, and probably was.
There is also a *Field Service Pocket Book*, not well-thumbed,
for, like the book on penguins lent to the little American girl,
it tried to tell me more than I wished to know. There is a *Field
Message Book*, which starts hopefully at one end with the
names and numbers of men in No. 5 Platoon and even more
hopefully at the other end with pencilled verses beginning 'I
stand for ever in the shadow of your hair, I am drowned in the
sleepy laughter of your eyes', and has nothing whatever
between these extremes, not a single message to anybody.
And now, these things out of the way, the Armistice is
celebrated, then merely hoped for; the guns roar, the guns roll
up, preparing to roar; the third time at the Front is followed
by the second, then the first; training ends, training begins;

Your King and Country Need You; the War breaks out, the War is not thought of; and I am back in that other world, taking the Duckworth Lane tram between Swan Arcade and my attic room.

On top of this little pile of Swan Arcadiana are some scribbling books I made myself at the office, when nobody was looking, probably between 1.15 and 1.45. Each has about fifty pages, eight inches by five, bound in the brown oiled sheets we used in the copying press. They are still holding together, these did-it-myself books, after half a century. I never wrote at a desk or on a table in my attic, always on my knee in an arm-chair close to the gas-fire, wondering if I ought to take my shins off the grill even if my hands would then be too cold. For knee-work these scribbling books were just right, not too thick and heavy, neither too stiff nor too flexible. I always wrote in them with a pencil; indeed, I cannot remember having a fountain pen before the First War. The pages I have looked at are almost dark with closely-pencilled lines, probably running to several hundred words a page. I find them difficult to read, these pages, and do not propose to try very hard; I also find them impressive, rather frightening. Was the boy the better man? As I have already suggested, I never think of myself as an energetic and determined man, living as I do behind some such *persona* in an interior atmosphere of laziness and irresolution. But these pages, with about eight lines of pencilling to an inch, show me a lad bent on writing – and after a long day in an office too – even if he ruined his eye-sight and burnt the skin off his shinbones. Nobody wanted this stuff he was writing; he was not meeting a demand. On the other hand, he did not believe he was a genius, did not see himself being driven by his daimon. Yet he had to sit up there, scribbling and scribbling away; and never out of boredom or for want of something more amusing to do, but resisting in-

numerable temptations to fleet the time elsewhere. I marvel a
the lad. What did he think he was doing?

One thing I do know about him, not having entirely lost
contact with my earlier self: he was not enormously ambitious, had no opulent spectacular daydreams. It may seem
odd, for at no time have I been without imagination, but I have
never been a daydreamer on the familiar grand scale. Even as a
boy I had never seen myself saving the life of some exquisite
girl, daughter of a duke or millionaire, who would afterwards
dote on me. As a useful soccer-player, always at full back, I had
never imagined myself keeping Everton or Aston Villa out of
the penalty area, amazing and delighting the Cup Final crowd
at Crystal Palace. I am certain that I never opened one of these
scribbling books and started pencilling away with the idea of
turning myself into 'the author of the season', as they said
then. I was a severely limited, almost humdrum, daydreamer.
No ambition fierce as that gas-fire burned in me. What I
imagined was only something nearly within my reach. What I
wanted then, I remember, was to live alone, though no doubt
amiable red-cheeked girls were not inaccessible, in one of
those ninepence-a-week cottages on the edge of the moors,
able to earn from writing the six, five, even four pounds a
month on which, in those days, I could easily keep myself.
Independence, not success and fame, was my dream. I do not
mean to suggest I was an austere character; I have always
been amiably self-indulgent, anything but iron-willed; but it is
a fact that I indulged in no huge romantic dreams, simply
wanted independence and to start my life as a professional
writer. (Indolent and irresolute I may be, as indeed I believe,
but there is a stubbornly independent streak in my nature: I
can be flattered and cajoled into making an ass of myself, but
not bullied.) Possibly laziness welcomed the prospect of
independence too. I saw myself in a dressing-gown, smoking a

pipe, when clerkdom was already pinned to its high stool for the day, toiling through to the moment when it could ask, 'Anything more, sir?' 'To hell,' I must have said, 'with all that', as I lit the attic fire and got out the scribbling books and the pencils.

Underneath these books in the pile of Swan Arcadiana – and I am not faking this but genuinely taking things as they come – is a typewritten piece with a covering of brown paper. It is headed *Moorton Sketches*. The subtitle describing this particular piece is *At the Music-hall,* to which is added hopefully *by J. Boynton Priestley, 5 Saltburn Place, Bradford, Yorks.* How many of these sketches I planned to do, I cannot remember now. I am ready to swear, however, that it was far more than I actually did do. Sketches of this sort were popular then but disappeared from periodical print long ago; some editor might well try reviving the form, so long as he could find specimens of it far better than mine seem to have been. The idea was that you described, briefly and from a lofty height of disdain, what was happening in the chosen place, like the music-hall in this sketch, and gave your readers snatches of dialogue, always done in dramatic form, between easily recognised types. Here we have, in the stalls, *Youth with Blue Collar* and *Pimply Youth, Fluffy-haired Girl* and *Lanky Male Companion, Youth with Big Bow-tie* and *Youth Smoking Russian Cigarette;* in the pit *Man in Tweed Cap* and *Neighbour,* and *Red-faced Girl* and *Surly Fiancé;* and in the gallery *Old Man* and *Man with Calabash Pipe,* and so on. The talk itself is better left within its brown paper covers; a candid account of one's distant youth should not be allowed to descend to masochistic exhibitionism. Nobody printed that sketch, *At the Music-hall.* There was no reason why anybody should have done. Possibly there is that famous 'promise' somewhere here; it seems to me hard to find. Any school magazine can improve on what is here;

only in the attempt to write the thing at all do I find *something*, not much but *something*.

If I were a lad of that age now, I suppose I would be dashing away at playwriting, unworried by lack of experience and any knowledge of stagecraft, already condemned on several Sundays by critics determined to be in the movement. Fifty years ago, however, it never occurred to me to attempt even a one-act play, for which there was then more demand, 'curtain-raisers' not having been banished. (There was a lot to be said for them: they took care of latecomers; they offered chances to young writers and actors; they helped playwrights to resist the temptation to pad out a good little dramatic idea into three acts.) Not that I was removed from the theatre itself. I was a constant and enthusiastic playgoer, defying the heat and discomfort of those old galleries. I enjoyed almost everything, from *Oedipus Rex* and *The Trojan Women* to the *Waltz Dream* and *The Count of Luxemburg* and *The Merry Widow*, of course, though, for some reason I have forgotten now, it was never one of my favourite Viennese operettas, all of which, incidentally, had real scores and orchestras, not just a night-club noise. I cannot say I enjoyed everything; I had reservations about a certain type of gentlemanly melodrama then in vogue: I remember one called *A White Man*. Appearing at the Theatre Royal, between Benson's Shakespeare and Edward Compton's Sheridan and Goldsmith, these pieces seemed contrived and anæmic, inferior to the full-blooded melodrama we had every week at the other theatre, the Prince's – *A Royal Divorce*, *The Face at the Window*, and the like. Yes, in my teens I could be said to be stage-struck, and it was an advantage to me long afterwards, when I came to work in the theatre, that I had left this complaint far behind, like the measles and mumps of my childhood.

The Theatre itself, however, was much further removed

from me then than it is from a teenager now. Except for that foreshortened but brilliant view we had from the gallery, it belonged to another world, closed to us. The gallery queue, where I waited many a freezing hour, used to extend towards the stage door, so that I often saw the actors, usually wearing gigantic overcoats, making their way there, perhaps loudly discussing professional topics. More than twenty years later, I sketched a portrait of one of them, Charlie Appleby in *Eden End*, but not out of any contemporary experience of him and his kind. The actors then were almost visitors from outer space. I could not imagine them in their digs, drinking bottled beer and eating ham and eggs. Actresses, wickedly painted even off the stage, were even more remote, hardly related biologically to the women and girls one knew, belonging to other orders of being, fays and sylphs and hamadryads. The whole business and interior traffic of the Theatre were unimaginable then; managements and agents and contracts, runs in the West End, bookings for Number One and Number Two tours, authors' royalties of five, seven-and-a-half, ten per cent of the gross, all were beyond the reach of knowledge, not even to be imagined. Is it surprising then that although I was a playgoer I never even thought of attempting a play? It would have been like writing something for King George and Queen Mary, newly crowned, and posting it off, with stamped addressed envelope for its return, to Buckingham Palace: not a rewarding idea at any time.

The next items of Swan Arcadiana suggest a closer approach to *Eng. Lit.* They are all in verse, of one sort and another. The first in this pile must in fact belong to the later years of this pre-1914 period. It is neither in typescript nor pencil but a fair copy in ink and print hand that I did myself, toiling out of love for the thing, for I cannot remember making such a copy of anything else. It is a narrative poem in blank verse, running to about a hundred and fifty lines: *Lancelot: After the Burial of Guenevere*. Why I chose this subject for what must have been my most ambitious performance, I do not know. I had read Malory, of course, and the various Arthurian poems of Tennyson, Morris, Swinburne; but was at no time bewitched by mediæval romance as so many persons have been. Indeed, I find some of the tales more fascinating now, when I begin to understand, with some help, the mythical and symbolic elements in them, their psychological depth. I also find it odd, now that I come to think of it, that no English prose writer of great talent has followed the poets to the Arthurian cycle, re-telling and expanding the tales as writers elsewhere have done with Greek, Norse, Irish myths and legends. I am certain, however, that young Jack Priestley was not so emotionally involved with Lancelot and Guinevere that he could only free himself through narrative in blank verse. He was, I am afraid, making use of them in a poetical exercise. It was the versifying, not what the versifying was about, that claimed him; there was a lack of an integrating, creative, truly poetic process in that attic; he was – let it come out – no poet.

Reading it again, I see now what all the combined efforts of all the weekly reviewers would not have made me see then, that this is the work of a youth who has read a lot of poetry, who is beginning to use words rhetorically, who is not a poet and never will be. But let us be clear – if only for a change – about poetry and poets. We English have certain terms to which we attach two different sets of meanings. They often involve us, innocently unless we are politicians or Establishment eulogists, in various kinds of double-talk. I have already suggested how this happens with *education*. There is the same confusion with *poetry*. It is true to say that young Jack Priestley will never write poetry. It is not true to say there is no poetry in him, as there was not, for example, in Jeremy

Bentham and Herbert Spencer. To write poetry, as distinct from mere verse, a man must be able to go mad while still keeping himself saner than most men; there must in fact be a certain relation between his conscious mind and his unconscious that I think I could explain, given the right opportunity and an adequate fee, but need not bother with here. Young Jack P. does not possess this sort of mind, a very rare sort, and never can acquire it. But in the larger non-literary sense of the term, he is full of poetry, being ardent and generous-minded, unashamed of his emotions, imaginative; and so, I declare very firmly, he will remain. We ought always to be aware of this confusion of meanings. For example, what is a critic trying to say when he tells us that what the English Theatre needs is more poetry? Does he mean there ought to be more plays written in rhymed or blank verse? Or does he mean that plays still written in prose should be less afraid of emotion, both larger and warmer, altogether more imaginative? He may know; we don't.

Rhetoric is what happens when a prose mind, moved by that other poetry which belongs to temperament not to literature, attempts the literary poetical. This blank verse piece about Lancelot is full of it, together with many echoes and bits of unconscious plagiarism. As for example—

> . . . . 'Sir Bors,' he said,
> 'This is the end. There is no loveliness
> Left in the light of day. God can throw down
> His baton to the starry floor, and sign
> For the long-dreaded withering of the world.'

Or this, from the same speech:

> '. . . . Arthur came
> From nowhere to a throne, and no man knows

Where he has gone. The common human cries
To him were but the twittering of birds;
All his great kingly life passed like a dream
Within a dream: the silken coloured show
And pomp of courts, the brazen trumpeting
And iron clamour of the lists at Camelot,
The hundred battles that once reeled and swayed
Beneath the dragon-standard, these to him
Were but dim shadowings and phantasies
Shifting and changing to the music made
By secret fairy lutes . . .'

Or again, just once more:

'If great love be a sin, then Hell is brimmed
With nobleness, and the high halls of Heaven
Are crowded with cold-handed bargainers
And steel-mouthed women . . .'

I do not need to be told that the purely literary value could be
worked out at about the equivalent of a penny a line. Taken
away from cold print, rolled out by a handsome actor, artfully
costumed and lit, some of these lines might come to life in a
theatrical fashion, perhaps more successfully than the dramatic
work of real poets who should never have left the printed page.
The dilemma of our poets, when they enter the Theatre, is
that either they must write below their reputations or risk
being incomprehensible at a first hearing, and then have little
chance of being given a second and third hearing by baffled
audiences.

The next piece of verse, neatly typed – certainly not by me,
by one of the girls – on very thin paper now sadly crumpled,
consists of seven eight-line rhymed stanzas, and is called

Evensong to Atlantis. It is very bad indeed; I can never have done worse. The subject must have clouded such judgment and self-criticism as I possessed. Around 1911 and 1912 I was haunted by the idea of Atlantis, to which I devoted many verses. To tell the truth, a little of this old fascination still lingers, surviving the affectionate derision of an archæologist and prehistorian very close to me. But why, fifty years ago, when I was no theosophist, no admiring student of Besant and Leadbeater, was I captured by this idea of Atlantis, the great civilisation that perished? What was there in my unconscious – and an almost magical infatuation of this kind must involve the unconscious – that responded at once to the legend? And I seem to remember, though I may be cheating a bit, that I was not held by the idea of a whole civilisation destroyed by natural causes, some shift in the ocean floor, some volcanic upheaval, but by the opposing and more subtle idea that Atlantis destroyed itself, its black-robed high priests serving only knowledge and power. And what was it that leapt out of the dark of my own mind to accept, to welcome, this legend? We assume that legends and myths, so far as they have any connection with historical time, point back to some remote age when they themselves took shape. But what if a few of them point the other way? Suppose the destruction of Atlantis had not happened but was going to happen? We were not leaving it behind but rushing towards it, perhaps; so that sitting up there in my attic, before life claimed too much of me, closing the little window still open then in the shadowy half of my mind, I found myself wondering over and over again about Atlantis. There are patterns of cause and effect we do not understand, so we pretend they do not exist, keeping even a glimpse or a hint of them out of all textbooks. It seems to me that the teenage versifier of Atlantis themes, fifty years away, and the elderly writer I know so much better, dragging himself on to platforms to speak about nuclear disarmament, are related in more ways than one.

The third poem, if I may call it that, is on stouter paper and typewritten too, and I think I did this fair copy myself at the office. It is a short piece of free verse, entitled *The Song of a Mood*. 'Tonight,' it begins, 'I think the world is dying.' And the first stanza ends with the 'Women of all ages' stitching a shroud, the second with the 'Heroes of all ages' digging a grave, the third with the 'Poets of all ages' singing a requiem. Not as awful as that *Evensong*, but not good. But here again, we may well ask, why this particular theme, even at seventeen and spending too many hours on an office stool? I was no sickly over-introverted youth, hiding behind lace curtains on a small regular income. I was in fact an extremely robust lad, a loud emphatic talker, a notable clown at parties, who had grown up and was still living in what we regard now as a golden age of security. Why did I, with so many interests, so much to do, spend time and trouble on a lament for a dying world? Had I guessed somehow that the world I was in fact enjoying, my world, to which part of me belongs yet, was indeed very near its end, that in a few years it would have gone for ever? I ask these questions like the men who produce television documentaries on urgent social problems. And like them I have no answers.

I sent this *Song of a Mood*, together with others I have forgotten, to 'AE' (George Russell) in Dublin. It was the first time I had ever done such a thing; and I think, though I am open to correction, that this first time was also the last, for later, after the War, unlike many young writers then, I never sent manuscripts in this fashion to older established authors, never tried to interest them in what I was doing. Why I chose Russell, I do not know. Possibly I had been reading his own verse; probably I admired the figure that emerged, the only one there not caricatured, in George Moore's *Ave*, which had just been published. The verses came back with a four-page letter that is at my elbow now as I write this; no date on it, only *Monday*; and it is in a hand full of character and obviously rapid and not easy to decipher, so that I may have to guess at a word here and there:

I was greatly interested in your poems. The *Song of a Mood* is, I think, very beautiful and imaginative and is also better in form than the others. You have obviously imagination and feeling but you have not yet mastered the form. If you are repelled from the archaic forms of verse rhyme and accent and feel you must write in free metres I would advise you to keep continuously in mind the more lyrical parts of the old English translation of the Bible, also Walt Whitman at his best. In the best of these the sense of balance and rhythm is perfect in the sentences and with the memory of these you might be able to make the unrhymed irregular metres sing. [He then quotes with approval the slightly varied refrain in my *Song of a Mood*.] This repetition is the intellectual equivalent of rhyme or measured verse and begets in the mind the idea of form and it satisfies one. My criticism is merely a technical one because technique is the only thing in which one writer can really advise another. No one can give another imagination, but the craft can be passed on and it is there, I think, you are most deficient. You should try by study of the best models to get your ear more sensitive to the balance of sentences so that you will feel instinctively where the verse ought to end. It makes all the difference between a sentence which lingers singing in one's memory and a sentence which we forget because it is formless and does not harmonise with the [three words I cannot decipher here] music in ourselves. I think you have a poetic vision and I hope you will go on writing and try above all to cultivate the intensity of will as well as the intensity of vision, because the will is the begetter of music and rhythm even as the vision is the begetter of thought. I thank you for your kind letter and for letting me see your verses. I would be glad later on to see more of your work, especially if you have things as fine as the *Song of a Mood*.

How many hundreds of letters like that Russell wrote, God knows – or perhaps some recording angel he caught a glimpse of while painting water-colours one week-end. He was far from being great in painting, poetry, criticism; yet he was undoubtedly a great man; a triumphant proof of the idea that so long as a man guards against intolerance and anger, it is better to believe in too much than to believe in too little. He was one of those who seem to spend a life with us almost in innocent bewilderment, because they come from some larger, nobler race. He had some economic and political ideas that are not behind our time but ahead of it; he proved himself a more practical man than the hard-headed realists; and during the years when Ireland was at war with the British Government and then with herself it was to this seer, this poet and painter of gods, demigods, angels, fairies, that men turned in the dark and confusion, aware then of his strength, his steadfastness. One of his favourite beliefs was that in this age we have disinherited ourselves. As he wrote to a friend: 'We have imagined ourselves into littleness, darkness and ignorance, and we have to imagine ourselves back into light.' That was thirty years ago; nothing much has happened since to prove he was wrong.

I continued to write verse of various kinds, though neither steadily nor in great blazing spurts, until about the end of the

First War. This did me much good, no harm; for in spite of the fact that while I was in the Army I wrote hardly anything but occasional verse, when I left it I could write a page or two of readable prose, whereas up to 1914, as I see now, what I wrote in any prose form was quite shockingly bad. At Cambridge, after the War, I amused myself writing epigrams, which got into print and even crept into an anthology or two. (No harm in them, unlike any appearance in school books, convincing the brightest boys and girls you are a dreary old codger, not worth reading out of school hours.) By that time, however, I knew I was no poet. This was disappointing; I believed – and still do – that poets are best, the real top people. They have to be very good, however, and third-rate poets must fall in behind writers of honest prose.

The remaining items in this collection of pre-1914 stuff prove that I was a long way from any claim to be considered a writer of honest prose. It is curious what happens when I look at these typescripts. The sense of identity with this lad vanishes. When I think about his life, it is my life that returns to memory; I feel I have moved on to another and much later chapter, but obviously it is all one chronicle. On the other hand, these stories, sketches, articles, do not seem to belong to me at all. Perhaps because I am ashamed of them, all connection with them has been broken. I cannot remember writing them. I might be looking at anybody's first attempts. No editor can have rejected them more coldly and completely than I do now. The lad who wrote them does not seem to me to reveal any talent at all, not even a glimmer of 'promise'; he is remarkable among junior clerks only because he insists upon trying, filling page after page of notebooks with his close pencil scrawls, bullying or begging his girl-friends to type them out for him, plugging away. Yet in my professional life, beginning about ten years after this time, I have been anything but ambitious, determined, dedicated to some idea of achievement; I have in fact been fertile but careless, never working to a plan, never really conscious, as many writers are, of being responsible for a literary career. This lad of 1911 is myself; I can remember almost exactly what he thought and felt on many occasions, and indeed can re-live some of his moments, as if time were reversible. Yet this extraordinary change occurred, from obstinate plodding to rather careless rapid performance, apparently a change in character and not simply a gain in ability; and now I am asking myself when it happened. Was it some time – even though I did hardly any writing then – in the First War? Was there some shift in the depths because I survived the massacre, unlike most of the young men I knew? Possibly, possibly not, as Cyril Joad was so fond of saying.

In this final batch of stuff there is another Moorton Sketch, *At the Pantomime*, better ignored. There is also one of those 'mood pieces' fairly common in those days, so that this specimen found its way into print. It is called *A Nocturne*, and begins:

You tak' the high road an' I'll tak' the low road, sang the old man, with trembling fingers adding a feeble obbligato on his violin. He stood underneath a street-lamp, and the sickly pale-green rays were merciful – for the gloom was thick. Here and there the faint light was reflected in little pools and puddles in the road, and the old man's boots squelched ominously at every movement. Everything was dark and wet. Even the rain seemed to be black and unclean, as if the heavens had long ago tried to sweeten the place and failed miserably . . .

and goes on, with glimpses of dreadful interiors, through a thickness of gloom that could be described with relish only by a robust and high-spirited youth. Had I seen and heard that old man, and the little thin man 'clad in steaming rags' who spat convulsively, and the coarse fat woman, like a pig, who grunted and snorted, and the three children trying to sleep in a corner of the hovel that was 'a chaos of filthy refuse' ? I had not. I was making it all up as my shins got hotter and hotter in the attic.

There are three short stories – that is, here properly typed out, for there are others in the scribbling books, smudged and hard to decipher – and I have just read them. Even as teenage attempts they seem to me to have hardly any merit. One is called *An Excess of Discipline*. It is based on the idea, which I certainly did not discover, that one way of defeating a justifiable complaint to authority is to smother it beneath a number of frivolous complaints about the same person. So in this story the second mate cannot make the skipper listen to his charge against the sailor Tomlin, who struck him, because Tomlin's shipmates have already been to the skipper with silly complaints against him. Where or from whom I borrowed this idea, I cannot remember now, but undoubtedly it was not mine. I knew nothing about life aboard small ships, and I must have chosen this setting under the influence of W. W. Jacobs, a great favourite of my father's. I was fond of Jacobs too, and in the early Twenties I wrote a critical appreciation of his work for the *London Mercury* and had some talk with him later – he was a small, neat man, like a shy chief clerk – in some club, probably the Garrick. He was as much undervalued by the intelligentsia as Wodehouse, no funnier and less adroit and inventive, was over-praised by them. Both were limited and highly artificial humorists, but it seems to me that Jacobs, in his dry fashion, was a far more ingenious plotter and came closer to those enduring weaknesses of human nature displayed in all good comedy. Perhaps he found less favour with the English educated classes because, unlike

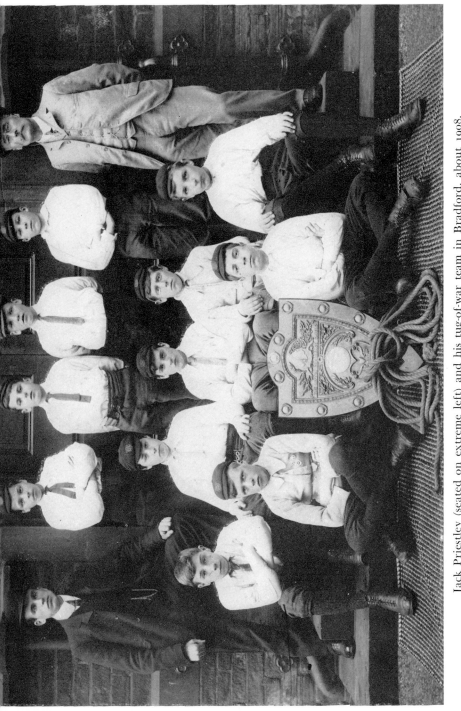

Jack Priestley (seated on extreme left) and his tug-of-war team in Bradford, about 1908.

As a lance corporal, just before going to the Western Front in 1915.

The prisoner-of-war camp football team with the author sitting on the major's left.

What the British front line was like in the winter of 1915-16. (*Imperial War Museum*)

J. B. Priestley and Beatrice Lillie painting the crease for a benefit cricket match

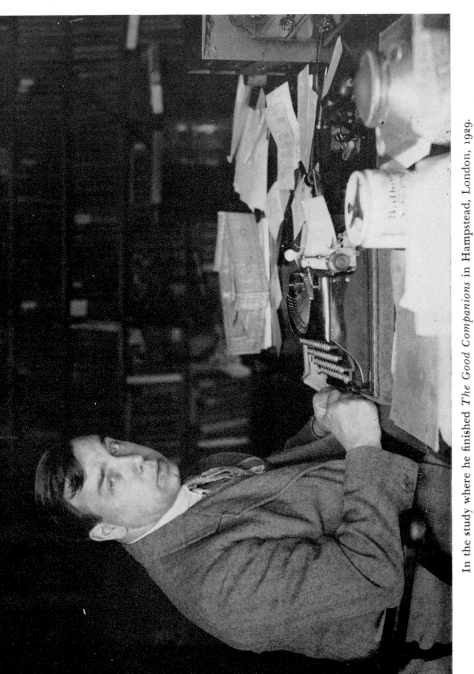

In the study where he finished *The Good Companions* in Hampstead, London, 1929.

The author in 1930.

Owned and occupied by J. B. Priestley for ten years beginning in 1931, No. 3, The Grove, Highgate Village, was the house where Coleridge lived and died.

J. B. Priestley with Ronald Colman in a Hollywood studio, spring, 1931.

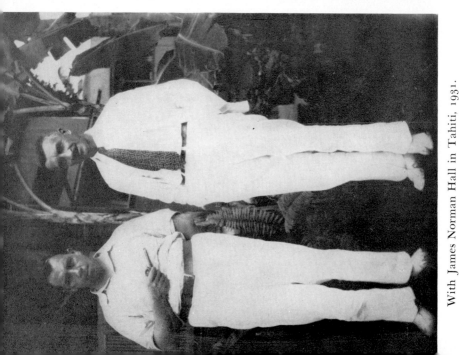

With James Norman Hall in Tahiti, 1931.

Billingham Manor, Isle of Wight, where Mr. Priestley did most of his work during the 1930s. His study was the top room with the curved side windows.

With George Bernard Shaw and John Drinkwater at Malvern, 1931.

J. M. Barrie with two of J. B. P.'s daughters. Taken in the garden of 3, The Grove, Highgate Village, in the early Thirties.

On 'Marble' the mule, at the bottom of the Grand Canyon in the mid Thirties.

J. B. Priestley as Henry Ormonroyd in *When We Are Married* early in its London run, 1938-39.

A bust by Jacob Epstein now in the J. B. Priestley collection of the Humanities Research Center, the University of Texas.

Broadcasting during World War II.

A recent photograph—at the gate of Kissing Tree House near Stratford-on-Avon.

J. B. Priestley and his wife, Jacquetta Hawkes.

Wodehouse, he did not write as if he had never left school.

The second story, *The Way In*, is longer but not much stronger. A young clerk goes to the nearest big town but cannot get a job in an office and has no chance of showing what he can do as an entertainer at the piano. (What has become of these entertainers? It is years since I last saw and heard one.) Finally – and unconvincingly, I am afraid – he is given a chance to deputise for a popular light comedian at the local music-hall, because in fact he has sneaked into the orchestra pit and there collected and hidden away the light comedian's band parts. This is not as wildly improbable as it first appears to be, for the youth had already been engaged at this music-hall as a 'walk on'. What happens now I do not know, but in the provinces at this time touring managers often employed, usually for a shilling or two a night, local youths as 'supers', and somewhere among my essays is one describing how I appeared in a Beecham touring production of Gounod's *Romeo and Juliet* as a member of the Town Guard of Verona. Less theatrically ambitious and rougher lads became 'gallery boys' during the run of a pantomime; they were paid nothing but were given free admittance into the gallery corners, where they led the applause and the chorus singing and generally served as a claque. They cannot be compared of course with the drilled and highly specialised claques of the continental theatres, where one group would be trained to lose all control, jumping up to wave and to cheer, another group, scattered among the audience, would gasp or sigh, others would weep audibly during scenes of pathos. Far removed from such expert performers were our gallery boys, packed into those spaces where they could see hardly anything at all; they played their humble parts by ear. I knew all about them because a cousin of mine was one of them year after year, a true 'corner boy'. It was he who told me, when I was about fourteen and distantly infatuated with the principal girl, Mabel Sealby, that she might be soon leaving the pantomime, weeks before it was due to close; and I remember how miserable I felt then, how such light as Bradford had in January retreated before sudden shades of darkness.

Reading *The Way In* again, long after I have forgotten how I came to write it at all, by keeping sympathy at a full stretch I can find just a touch or two, though nothing worth quoting, that might suggest I could write readable fiction some day. In one passage the youth, still without a job and now short of money, catches sight of his reflection in a milliner's window and realises that already 'an indefinable air of shabbiness' is pervading his appearance. What I did not know then is that at any time during the next fifty years, when I caught sight of myself unexpectedly anywhere, I would be as dismally surprised. I suspect now that the struggle to tell the tale in any acceptable fashion, even to string the sentences together, made such demands that I could not bring each little scene to life. Without having to make such an effort, just talking it to somebody, I would have done much better; which probably explains why I appeared then to impress my company, certainly if they were contemporaries, more forcibly than anything here on paper suggests. But then the real work, at that early stage, was not being done on paper but in my head, for, though I remember so little about this actual writing, I have a fairly clear recollection of the way in which I would observe and speculate about other people and then combine the results of these processes with such self-knowledge as I possessed. When enough of these ingredients has been assembled and the mixing has gone on for years, not on a conscious but an unconscious level, then, when the words can be commanded at last, a man gives himself a chance to create fiction or drama. The idea and the shaping of it may be new, but the material of novel or play placed at the service of the idea, the basic stuff that has to be shaped, is delivered from some central store, the mind having crammed it full after years of observing and speculating both outside and inside. A writer of fiction or drama is fortunate in one respect, that although in a sense he never stops working, that is, accumulating this raw material, he is also amusing himself all the time, a hundred fragments of narrative, sketchy scenes probably involving the people he has to meet, hurrying through his head all day. When I wrote stories like these, I had only just begun, had not enough of this essential mixed stuff; now, when I am almost out at the other end, with the warehouse no longer piled high, when the mixing processes themselves are becoming wearisome, perhaps the words that are written are better than what they have to tell. That young self and this one, here and now, look at each other and exchange grins, while another self, committed to neither of them, not to authorship, hardly to life on this planet, possibly manages a tiny ironical smile.

The third of these stories, *Poor Old Dad*, is no better than the other two, perhaps worse, but is not entirely without interest. It begins:

Henry Copestrake was a well-known figure in Moorton and district, and residents often pointed him out to strangers as 'the famous artist'. The adjective was too flattering, for Copestrake was not a famous artist and never had been. When he was younger he had a certain reputation as a painter of scenes and characters from Celtic mythology, and had been frequently hung in the Royal Academy, many of his pictures fetching large prices, but his work was only an aftermath of the Pre-Raphaelites, and now he was forgotten by all but a few of the older art critics and of course his neighbours at Moorton . . .

There is a good deal more, showing us his pointed beard, fine aquiline nose, his lofty forehead and light blue eyes, his old Norfolk jacket, black soft felt hat, perpetual pipe, before he and the story, if it can be called one, move an inch. He married a shrewd, capable North Country woman, who died when their only son, George, was only ten. It is George now who takes over. He goes to the Moorton Grammar School, does well there too, but then astounds his father by declaring that he does not want to be a painter, to wear a Norfolk jacket and black soft felt hat, to read Ruskin and William Morris: he wants to go into business. Within ten years he is making big money; he marries the daughter of one of the richest manufacturers in Moorton; for him there is room at the top. His father, now running to seed and whisky but with his idealism still untarnished, invests what is left of his savings in an arty weekly that will lead 'a crusade against Modern Commercialism'. George tells his father that this paper will not run a month. George is right, of course; old Henry Copestrake, no longer a famous artist, is ruined. But he refuses any help from his son, whose way of life he denounces in the first and worst of many such speeches I seem to have written; and he shambles, though not entirely without dignity, out of the story, 'to teach art at a boarding school in North Yorkshire' – probably Dothegirls Hall. The George Copestrakes, one of them 'wrinkling her pretty brows', cannot understand the old man; just as I cannot understand why I thought this melancholy chronicle, in which there might have been a novel of sorts if I had known more about the people, would be welcomed anywhere as a short story.

What interests me now, however, has nothing to do with the craft of fiction. It is what I made the ambitious George do, so long ago. Out of my distant innocence, as round and complete and new as a fresh egg, I wrote:

Just at that time, England was invaded by a swarm of agents of the American Correspondence School, and very soon some of them reached Moorton. Posters were plastered all over the town – striking American posters with cryptic messages and glowing pictures of Unsuccessful Men, unshaven and wearing dilapidated boots, and Successful Men with big chins and frock-coats. Every poster prominently displayed the well-known motto of the American Correspondence School – *Get on or Get out*. George was fascinated and, after a little persuasion from one of the cigar-smoking agents, agreed to take a two years' special course in advertising . . .

Then George becomes an advertising agent, and very soon a successful one too. Though I knew nothing about this business, I did not shrink from describing how he succeeded in it, sketching his campaigns to boost sweetmeats, boot polish, picture palaces, keeping up a refrain of *Ideas! Ideas! Ideas!* George, after establishing branches of his agency in other northern towns, became known as 'The Boomer'. All this astonishes me now. Until I re-read this story, after such a long interval, I had forgotten that the advertising fuss was already on then, that I had my eighteen-year-old eye on it, that already in those lost afternoons we were moving towards what I have since called Admass. As a short story *Poor Old Dad* is a miserable effort, best forgotten, but as a tiny piece of social history, at least in my record of it, we can say the thing just creeps home.

At the bottom of the pile, where they belong, are a few articles. They suggest that the J. Boynton Priestley who wrote them was about eighty years old, probably a retired clergyman. Dipping in, I find him declaring: 'To the average man one can say nothing'; not a statement likely to attract any newspaper editor. One of the subjects here, surprisingly enough, is the Cinema, then merely making a start, often still including a free cup of tea in its sixpenny charge of admission. But J. Boynton makes a bold frontal attack on his subject: 'When one thinks,' he writes, 'of the enormous multitudes daily enthralled by the Cinema, and of the power and influence it must therefore wield, it makes one wonder whether the people who present it to the public realise what a weapon they hold, for good or evil.' It does indeed, to this very day. J. Boynton's heart is in the right place here, but not his pen, which should be on the desk of some leader writer on a third-rate provincial paper. Even as early as this, he ought to have been doing better. The truth is, as I see now, I developed and matured very slowly, still not entirely out of the egg when lads younger than I was, a little later, had left all the shell behind and were pecking anything available. Though I wrote little during the First War, no doubt its experiences brought me nearer to some sort of maturity, not yet to be expressed in writing; but I remember how in 1919, when at last I was demobilised into a world strange to me, I was astonished by what seemed to me the cool precocity of my juniors, hardly out of school before they were writing and publishing volumes of verse, novels, reviews and criticism. I could not imagine how they had done it. Were they phenomenally brilliant or was I, for all my determination to write, rather stupid?

5

When I first began thinking about these years between leaving school and joining the Army in 1914, I made no distinction between them; this Swan Arcade time seemed all of a piece. Now when I have done a little exploring of the past, using no records of it, working entirely through memory, I see that there is a natural break between the first two years, when I was sixteen and seventeen, and the second two, eighteen and nineteen. (I enlisted a few days before I was twenty.) At my age, looking back a long way as I have to do now, the calendar has to be dismissed as a cheat. Those four years are not the sections of time I know now. Between the ages of sixteen and twenty we can experience more time than we shall ever recognise once past sixty, no matter how long we live. The rapid heartbeats of youth expand and diversify the years; a lot has happened to me since, say, 1941, but I seem to myself hardly different, whereas at nineteen I would have disowned and dismissed my sixteen-year-old self, a kid who had done nothing and been nowhere. So now I see that I am writing this while the house lights are up and there is an interval before the Second Act, opening some time in 1912.

It is true that the strongest lines in the pattern of living remain unbroken. I still lived at home, though in a more detached fashion, in Saltburn Place, Toller Lane. I still took the tram from Duckworth Lane to its terminus at the bottom of Sunbridge Road, and then walked along Market Street to Swan Arcade, pretending to be a junior clerk in a wool office. Both at home and at work the sets and the cast were the same; nevertheless, the play was different, going forward now in Act Two. No names have been changed, but here I am a different youth living in a different town. Before I come back to writing I will take the first example of this difference that comes to mind. By 1913, I remember now, I might or might not condescend to make an appearance at the summer band concerts in Lister Park. This indifference would have been unimaginable to me in 1911, when only rain that never looked like stopping could have kept me away. To be somewhere else, actually preferring the mere crumbs of existence, when the band would be playing in Lister Park – no, I could not have dreamt it of myself two years earlier.

These were no ordinary open-air concerts, not even on Wednesday nights, though these in turn were inferior to the Saturday performances, for which the finest military bands in the country were engaged. I imagine – and I do not say I know, not having any clear evidence – that such bands, notably those of the various Guards regiments and the Marines, were then at their best, the instrumentalists, musicians rather than soldiers, having been selected and trained during years of peace. They had no strings of course apart from a double-bass; the string parts were scored for woodwind, especially clarinets; and their programmes consisted of overtures, a few tone-poems, ballet suites, selections from grand and comic opera, and various catchy light pieces of the time. One of these last, always being played then, *In the Shadows*, still dances in my head and I wish I had a recording of it, performed by a military band. Nothing would bring back so quickly and truly the time, the scene, the moods of my youth, than the sound of *In the Shadows*. Austere musicians dismiss this flimsy tinkling too easily; so-called light music has its own value, not really-belonging to music at all. Because, unlike serious work, it lacks musical content, it acts as a series of vials, often charmingly shaped and coloured, for the distillations of memory. The first few bars of it remove the stopper; we find ourselves re-living, not remembering but magically recapturing, some exact moments of our past. At least that is how it is with me; a tune from a forgotten operetta, an old music-hall ditty, is my equivalent of Proust's *madeleine*.

My father and his friends were always among the thousands in the tiers of chairs that curved round the bandstand, though not entirely enclosing it. They were concert-going as well as sitting in the open, smoking their pipes; they could be critical, and were not to be brassed and cymballed into appreciation; and I have listened more than once to a close friend of my father's – a happy man who had a tiny business he could leave any time for expeditions and cricket matches, company and the discussion of fine points – explaining why the clarinets of the Scots Guards, his favourites, were superior to those of the Irish or the Coldstream. High above the nearest rows of chairs, higher than the top of the bandstand itself, was a promenade, and there the youth of our part of Bradford – Lister Park not being far from where I lived – congregated densely, some of the lads and girls packed along the rails, looking down through the blue haze of smoke and catching what came to them of *Coppélia* or *Les Deux Pigeons*, and all the rest, past counting, on the move in a thick sluggish stream, in which, as I realised more than once, it was devilish hard to find the only face you wanted. This innocent parade was often condemned by deacons and elders, who seemed to think that because they had had enough of it, all sexual life, together with all dressing-up, display, showing off, pursuit and capture, should come to an end. No doubt the young males were often merely predatory – though the worst of them never paraded in the park, but, like two older men I knew slightly, lurked else-where, bent on seducing half-witted housemaids – but the girls, wearing their best clothes and usually in arm-linked trios and quartets, must have known very well, in spite of their glad-eyeing, whispering and giggling, that it was here, not in the mill or the office, not even at home or at the chapel bazaar, they were engaged in the serious business of life. And the place and the hour were propitious for mating : a summer evening, trees and grass between youth and the dark narrow streets; the hills above the tree-tops fading into dusk; all the people, thousands and thousands of them, sitting, standing, or in the slow river of faces on the promenade; the lighted bandstand in the haze below, a glitter of instruments, the scarlet flash of a uniform, coming through the blue air, and music coming too, not recognisable, not attended to, a long way off, but music. A good place, a good time, for the beginning of love.

Not that love began for me there. Usually with a friend or two I would stand not far from the entrance to the chairs enclosure, which we never thought of entering because we did not consider these military band performances worthy of our continuous close attention. It was a sound tactical position: we were below and to one side of the packed promenade, yet not too near the bandstand where no girls could be seen. There we could keep an eye on almost everything and everybody, for the end of the parade was not far away, dropping down a little, widening and thinning out, near where most of the promenaders, as regular as sentries, turned to face their beat again. As I have already suggested, the glimpse of one particular face, unknown and fair, a flower among puddings, might send us wriggling and pushing through the throng to have another and better look. But then such faces could lure us into every quarter of the town, even into Sunday-night services in remote bethels, grim little fastnesses of primitive Methodism, where romantic profiles, wandering bright eyes, could not be forbidden. This quest and then pursuit of the face that haunted the teenage imagination, in those days when girls were still guarded and parents could arrive, even at a street corner, like sulphurous dragons, seem to me to have been overlooked by the older novelists of our industrial society, myself included; and now of course, when the youngsters are copulating at about the time we were beginning to hold hands, it is too late. What may be missed now, I suspect, even though I am not one of the head-shaking elders who denounce sexual looseness, is the result of a certain unfocused desire we experienced, known, I imagine, to girls at any time, that dammed up and heightened romantic feeling, male tenderness.

If I do not shake my head now, however, it is because I discovered so much during the second half of this period, when I went where I pleased as I had not done earlier, for then I was still too young to visit pubs and music-hall bars, to observe the town at night with its lid off. An ultra-respectable suburb like ours, I began to see, had too many badly divided men, all heavily solemn and frock-coated on Sunday morning, too coarsely raffish, well away from their families, on Saturday night. Managers who were obdurate if the mill girls wanted another shilling a week could be found in distant pubs turning the prettiest and weakest of them into tarts. (Over thirty years later I made some use of these discoveries in a play, *An Inspector Calls*, set in 1912.) It is true that the women and girls who worked in the mills then were no models of feminine refinement. Sometimes, when I finished earlier than usual at the office and walked home, the route I preferred took me past one of the largest mills in the district, often just when the women were coming out. I would find myself breasting a tide of shawls, and something about my innocent dandyism would set them screaming at me, and what I heard then, though I was never a prudish lad, made my cheeks burn. And it was still the custom, in some mills if not in that particular one, for the women to seize a newly-arrived lad and 'sun' him, that is, pull his trousers down and reveal his genitals. But all this not unwholesome and perhaps traditional female bawdiness – there was a suggestion of mythology, ancient worship, folklore, about that queer 'sunning' ritual – was far removed from cynical whoring. There was nothing sly, nothing hypocritical, about these coarse dames and screaming lasses, who were devoted to their own men, generally working in the same mill, and kept on 'courting', though the actual courtship stage was over early, for years and years until a baby was due, when they married. They may not have lived happily ever afterwards, but they saved themselves from some unpleasant surprises.

Elsewhere, however, the more I discovered in those two years or so, the more I felt I was tunnelling through a mountain of humbug and hypocrisy. Not that all the more raffish householders in our suburb were hypocrites. There was a type existing then that I imagine has largely vanished from later suburbs. This was the decent family man, at ordinary times a model husband, father, rate-payer, who would be suddenly compelled to break all the rules, dismissing all responsibilities, vanishing from home and office, unaccountably behaving like a gold-miner new from the diggings and going off on a tremendous 'binge', nobody knew where. The economics of these sudden compulsive sprees puzzled me. Even in those days, when drink was cheap, a week of boozing, standing treat in pubs wide open from early morning to night, rollicking and whoring around, must have cost a handful of golden sovereigns; yet these break-outs were never planned, immediately took a man away from banks and offices into low company unlikely to accept cheques, so how they were financed remains a mystery to me. Generally these revellers crept home at last in darkness, worn out. But not always, for I remember a neighbour of ours, normally a dapper and precise insurance broker, staggering home in the middle of the afternoon one week-end, looking solemn as a judge but carrying at arms' length an enormous fish. Another of these intermittent rebels, whom I knew, was an art dealer. I had forgotten his name, though I remembered his appearance, talk and habits, when a year or two ago a London dealer asked me if I had known him in Bradford, telling me that my old acquaintance had had a remarkable flair for good pictures, and had persuaded a few of his West Riding clients to let him buy for them, at prices that seem a maddening joke now, fine examples of the Impressionists and Post-Impressionists. This I did not know, fifty years ago, but I did know that this Bradford dealer would often suddenly disappear, not into Parisian *ateliers* but Yorkshire low life, returning after a week or so broke, mumbling, plastered in muck. Such men could keep going only if they had their own saturnalia from time to time, letting the *shadow* take over for a week.

There were more defiant and odder rebels. I remember a family friend, a brilliant high-spirited type, gloriously daft at parties, who had risen fast to become head cashier at a very large works. Then, with all set fair, when he looked like the kind of man we see in advertisements now, he had had some dispute with his employer, had considered himself unjustly treated, and had walked out. He had not walked out of this particular job to find another, he had said goodbye to the lot – regular employment, decent provision for wife and family, rents and rates and taxes, respectability, shaving and clean linen. To hell with them all! He picked up an odd job or two, a few hours a week, that just enabled him to get by; nobody, not even his wife, really knew how he lived; and now and again I came across him in the town – a long way from our suburban parties and whist drives – wearing an old straw hat, no tie and a frayed shirt, a week's beard, and a sardonic grin. The people who saw a fairly recent farcical comedy of mine, *Mr Kettle and Mrs Moon*, about a bank manager who suddenly decided one wet Monday that he had had enough, the people who thought I no longer cared about probability, ought to have known this Bradford man, who made my Mr Kettle look like a cautious experimenter. Indeed, Bradford before 1914, extreme Yorkshire provincialism mixed and leavened with German-Jewish liberalism in exile and other exotic elements (I used to walk past mercantile brass plates that read *Delius & Co.* then *Kafka, Rothenstein & Co.*), was a rum place. I have never done it justice. But manna fell on some of those cobbled streets, and I did not miss all of it, found a little divine nourishment here and there.

Occasionally we took a train to Leeds, only ten miles away and larger than Bradford, a city with law courts and a university and a main-line station but, in Bradford opinion, inferior in wealth, civic progress, character and interest. (Prejudice, of course, but not wildly absurd, at least not at that time, for it was Bradford not Leeds that gave the country so many persons of note in the arts and sciences, set Labour politically in motion, made the social experiments.) When we went to Leeds it was generally because we wanted more cosmopolitan entertainment. One evening there, hot and astonished in the Empire, we discovered ragtime, brought to us by three young Americans: Hedges Brothers and Jacobsen, they called themselves. It was as if we had been still living in the nineteenth century and then suddenly found the twentieth glaring and screaming at us. We were yanked into our own age, fascinating, jungle-haunted, monstrous. We were used to being sung at in music-halls in a robust and zestful fashion, but the syncopated frenzy of these three young Americans was something quite different; shining with sweat, they almost hung over the footlights, defying us to resist the rhythm, gradually hypnotising us, chanting and drumming us into another kind of life in which anything might happen. All right, what we were hearing for the first time was *Alexander's Ragtime Band*, *Waiting for the Robert E. Lee* and the rest, not forgetting, though its title has gone, that intoxicating refrain which went 'Fiddle up, yiddle up (BOM) on your violin'. All right, okay, so what? Well, I believe that at least in our time the more-than-popular song, irresistible to ordinary people everywhere, is prophetic. Out of the depths it suddenly reveals, great and terrible events will come: politicians and social historians do not keep their ears open in the right places. (They should listen now, however nauseating they find them, to the pop songs of the teenagers, so full of self-pity, so wandering and rootless and far removed from all public and national life, clinging so desperately to a sexual relationship, all expressing disinherited youth growing up with the Bomb.) Out of those twenty noisy minutes in a music-hall, so long ago, came fragmentary but prophetic outlines of the situation in which we find ourselves now, the menace to old Europe, the domination of America, the emergence of Africa, the end of confidence and any feeling of security, the nervous excitement, the frenzy, the underlying despair of our century. Of course I was not consciously aware of all this on that evening, only knew that here was something new, strange, curiously disturbing. But let us keep our ears and minds open. Hedges Brothers and Jacobsen, under another name, with different words, music, tones and gestures, may be starting again next week, sketching an outline of the year 2000.

It was that evening, I think, that encouraged me to write a topical skit, an imaginary interview called *Secrets of the Ragtime King*. I sent it to a popular weekly, *London Opinion*, whose editor promptly accepted it, printed it, paid me a guinea for it. (That guinea must not be despised; it could have bought twenty-one cloth-bound masterpieces, or nearly four pounds of good tobacco, or a week's holiday.) My father knew and cared nothing about ragtime and was no reader of *London Opinion*, but he was impressed by this break-through into print and money, brought out a box of cigars I had been rifling in secret for some time, invited me to take a Key West – I think that is what his favourites were called – and together we lit up and puffed away, men of the world. I remember we had not been getting along too well before then. The cautious and dubious side of my father, the nothing-about-him, hanky-panky, won't-carry-corn department, had been taking a gloomy view of my prospects. My appearance and behaviour – 'Somebody saw you half-carrying a girl down the road, the other night' – were alienating sound local opinion. One or two suggestions I had made about keeping most of my Swan Arcade pittance, to put myself on a semi-independent basis, had been sharply dismissed, with remarks about lodgers not being wanted at 5 Saltburn Place. I had made no attempt, after many warnings, to keep earlier hours and generally could not explain what on earth I'd been doing with myself until such a time. So this London triumph, tiny though it was, came none too soon. Doubts on his side, resentment on mine, temporarily disappeared in the smoke of our Key Wests.

On the very day that issue came out with my piece in it, I rode for once inside the tram, not up top as I usually did, and so I was able to notice that the woman sitting opposite was glancing through *London Opinion*. At any moment she might begin reading my contribution to it. She was not at all like any reader I had ever had in mind. She was a sourish, suspicious-looking woman, somewhere in her disappointing forties; obviously not one to light up on first meeting in print J. Boynton Priestley. In fact – and if there is a fact I am certain about in this confusing world, it is this fact – she turned over page after page, never being really held, let alone delighted, by any of them. At what exact moment she glanced at and then passed by the ragtime king, it was impossible for me to tell. Perhaps she was not a real person at all – and the fact that she looked so like thousands of middle-aged women, a sort of composite portrait, was suspicious – but a supernatural being, belonging to a very low order of guardian angel, masquerading there to check any swell of pride, to nip *hubris* in the bud. If that will not do, then she was there, right at the start, as a warning, telling me in effect that I was now faced with the English reading public, the audience, the melancholy patrons, the dubious customers. Now I could see for myself that any further efforts in this scribbling line even then – to say nothing of the time when women, children, mortgages, taxes, doctors' bills, grocers and tailors and wine merchants, would have to be kept or paid out of scribble – would call for not only determination but sheer damned effrontery.

What I remember better than I do this woman opposite, however, is my state of mind when I realised that at any moment she might be reading what I had written. Mixed in it confusedly were eagerness, pride, self-love, self-doubt, shame : three parts champagne or brandy to one part each of castor oil and wormwood. And never since then have I lost, let alone forgotten, the unique glory-and-sick flavour of this mixture; it is the brew that all men who have talent but not genius must taste until they die. We go on and on, not altogether for a flat twenty per cent at our publishers, or ten per cent of the gross in the playhouse, but tantalised and lured on by ideas and believing too that we must justify our existence. But because we have not genius and no daimon controls us, there in the mixer goes the gin of self-confidence, hopeful skill, pride, and there for ever following them go the bitters of doubt and shame. But this last, I think, needs some explanation. I do not mean that we are ashamed of ourselves because we feel we have done bad work, though this of course can happen. It is closer to the kind of shame that blushing tender maidens once felt in company. There is shyness in it, a shrinking from exhibiting ourselves, a respect too for other people's feelings. An out-and-out genius, daimon-driven, believes that other people exist to understand and appreciate whatever he may choose to create. If they refuse this responsibility, so much the worse for them, blind, deaf and damned. We men and women of talent could adopt this attitude, but if we did we would be false to our inner nature, the real self that tells us that other people exist in their own right, that we are claiming time and attention as valuable to them as ours are to us, that we have cleared a space and are now in the middle of it and had better be good. We may come to have some pride in our ideas and skill, industry and experience – and great genius may never stoop to consider such matters – but from first to last we are never really proud of our *selves*. Who are we, after all, to beat a drum when the market square is still crowded and there are rumours that war may break out again?

6

From early in 1913 until the autumn I scribbled my way into enough local printed paper to cover our warehouse floor. This was in addition to making a few appearances in periodicals with a national circulation. What happened was that from January to October I wrote a column entitled *Round the Hearth* for a little Labour weekly, the *Bradford Pioneer*. This was of course journalism of the humblest sort, and unpaid at that. Nobody made a penny out of this pioneering. Mine was the cultural department, filled with paragraphs about books and concerts and plays: the rest of the paper, I feel certain though I cannot recall any of it, was narrowly and fiercely political. Bradford, the birthplace of the Independent Labour Party, was one of the earliest socialist strongholds. My father and many, though not all, of his friends were socialists. They were not Marxists – and I doubt if there was a student of economics among them – but were all in the looser and warmer English tradition of socialism. This was largely unplanned, too vague, too hopeful, but it was able, as some intellectual improvements upon it have not been able, to generate enthusiasm. It could create an atmosphere in which immediate and fairly radical reforms seemed possible. It may have moved towards an impossible goal, but on the way it could do more good than harm. In this respect it was unlike those movements that produce and are ultimately led by dedicated revolutionaries, men of steel, who soon begin to hate everybody, even the very people they are trying to rescue from poverty and despair. I grew up in this English socialist tradition, and at heart I still believe in it. Liberalism is modern man's nearest approach to real civilisation; as soon as most of it was sneered away, the power men took over, the secret police arrived, torture came back. This old-fashioned English Left was liberalism with the starch out of it, the fire lit, the company it could assemble more varied, easier and warmer-hearted, not incapable of a song and a chorus. It was life-seeking, life-enhancing, a protest, perhaps too late, on behalf of the feminine principle.

I grew up listening to political argument – some children enjoy adult talk, and I was one of them – and later I joined in, for though I have never been a compulsive talker, I cannot keep silent long. But during these later teens I found myself in a position where I have remained more or less ever since. I was politically-minded to some extent but never able to put politics first, always repelled not attracted by the political life. There are various reasons why a youngster may find a political atmosphere and political activities irresistible: he may be a blazing fanatic; he may be hungry for power on any level; he may be ambitious without possessing any particular talent; he may delight in intrigue, happiest when arranging with Smith and Brown to keep out Robinson; and he may combine all these so that in the end, at our expense, he gets the jackpot. I was not at all this kind of youngster; I never joined and worked for any political organisation; and indeed, as I try to remember that time, I cannot hear myself on any occasion insisting upon a political argument. Yet I must have done, and my memory is at fault here, because of what happened when I sailed to Copenhagen.

This was in June 1913. Through the office I had been given a pass that entitled me to a berth on one of the small steamers, called 'butter boats', on a regular service between Goole and Copenhagen, where their chief cargo was indeed butter. Under this amiable arrangement you paid only for your food, half-a-crown a day. It was wonderful blue-and-gold weather; the North Sea was not quite a millpond but was friendly, twinkling; and I spent many an hour up near the prow, happily lost in this newly-made oceanic world, where the first landfall must be Eden. I had never been at sea before; I was enchanted. But I could neither entirely escape from the captain nor get along with him, as my fellow passenger, another junior clerk from somewhere with a free pass, did by agreeing with everything the old man said. This I found impossible to do, he came out with such claptrap. He was a bull-headed choleric Tory, one of those men who simplify social and political issues by not giving them any thought, who settle arguments by providing you with dummy opinions that they proceed to demolish. It would have been more sensible for an eighteen-year-old, not even a real passenger but only some kind of supercargo, to accept without protest whatever a skipper said in his own saloon. Possibly I tried, I cannot remember now; but I know that it was not long before I felt compelled to reply for the Left – reasonably and quietly, I hope. The captain, whose remarks on all subjects had probably never been challenged before in that saloon, was soon purple-faced, goggle-eyed and very angry. By the time we had passed from the Skagerrak into the Kattegat he was no longer speaking to me. (This seems bad to me even after all these years: quick anger soon forgotten can be tolerated; so can sulking without any noisy loss of temper;

not anger followed by sulking.) This was embarrassing, but I
forgot about him when I stared over the ship's side at Copenhagen. I looked down on scores of comfortable middle-aged
men smoking cigars whose appearance suggested they were
aldermen, and I was astonished to learn, not from the captain,
that in this small comparatively poor country these men
were dockers. Then I saw a thousand beautiful girls on
bicycles. I was eighteen; I had ten golden sovereigns in my
pocket; I was landing for the first time in a foreign country; I
was in the place that has now crept out of all the gazetteers,
one where no plane touches down, Wonderland.

By this time I knew it had to be writing or nothing.
Previously, though writing came first, I saw no reason why I
should not do some great acting and sooner or later conduct a
few symphony orchestras. These were possibilities, nothing
more, and I did not work on them as I did with writing. They
have not entirely vanished, still exist in some corner of my
mind. The conductor is a very tiny wraith, terrified of company, only venturing out when I am alone – or when I think
my wife, who has endured much of it, might tolerate yet
another dose of this peculiarly male idiocy – and the record-
player is filling the room with glorious sound. The actor has
more life in him and indeed has collaborated sometimes with
the writer. I still fancy myself as an actor. And not entirely
without reason: events bring confirmation. For example,
some years ago I was trying to persuade a film producer that
an idea I had for a rather tricky story would make a good film.
I would sketch out a sequence, not writing it for him to read,
and then ask him to come down to me in the country. There I
would begin acting it out for him. 'Marvellous!' he would cry.
'You must write it. Go ahead.' But then, a day or so later, he
would telephone from London to express certain deepening
doubts. I would suggest another visit, to consider a further

sequence; and the same thing happened again, and again and again. Finally he said, 'If you'd act all the parts, we'd make the picture. But as soon as I'm away from you, and thinking it over, the story won't jell.' I was not disappointed when at last he rejected the idea; the actor in me had enjoyed himself and had been appreciated and applauded by an expert.

There are things I do now, however, that I never even considered doing then. During the last few years I have never gone anywhere longer than a few days without taking with me a knapsack filled with gouache tubes, water pans and brushes, plenty of good tinted paper; and at home I have spent many an afternoon, in a happy dream of creation, painting in oils. But in those two years before the First War it never occurred to me even to attempt to sketch or paint. I was not cut off from the visual arts, though I did not really know much about them until much later. But I went to the Arts Club now and again and knew a few goodish water-colourists who painted up in the Dales. And into my own set, now widening fast, came some art students, two or three of the elect who had left the local school of art, having won scholarships to the Slade. One of them, an excitable chap, not the easiest of company when the café was thick with the bourgeoisie, would leap out of a reverie to shout 'Goya!', almost as if he had just caught sight of the Spanish master ordering coffee and sardines-on-toast. It was this Goya enthusiast who declared he had such a passion for Beethoven's music that he would not listen to anybody else's. But this grand intolerance demanded a better ear and knowledge of style than he possessed, so that when I told him I would play as best I could some Beethoven for him, and actually gave him some Schubert, he hailed it with delight. 'Beethoven – the only one worth listening to,' he yelled. 'Beethoven! And Goya! Bloody marvels!'

When these Slade types returned to us during vacations,

their accounts of their life in London, like the fiction of the old Spanish picaresque writers, were 'epics of starvation'. Some of us in Bradford had to cut it fine, but these holders of art scholarships had to cut it even finer. Two of them I knew decided once to save money, time, and trouble by making a stew that would last them a week. They took some large tin container they had acquired to their back room in Ampthill Square, filled it with scrag ends and bargain vegetables, and balanced it perilously on their small gas-burner. One clumsy move, and of course it happened, and their week's rations, now bones and liquid, were all over the floor, with not another meal in sight for days. Among many things they learnt in London, with drawing at the Slade at the head of them, was when and where, usually at the back door of various hotels and restaurants, very early in the morning, to exchange a few pennies for a quantity of food, all gone stale but still eatable and possibly nourishing. A Bradford-to-Slade man I knew lived with his girl, also an art student, scratching along like two mice in a hard winter; but then by the end of the following year, after assuming that a contract they had been given really came out of the Arabian Nights, were occupying a large furnished villa and being waited upon by several domestics. Why are we told that Murger's *Vie de Bohême* is either fantasy or at best an account of life as a few young people knew it in Paris in the 1840s? Something very much like it seems to me to have gone on, never stopping, in many cities. In London now, however, the art student or penniless young writer is better placed than my friends were in 1913: there are part-time jobs to be had, washing up, serving drinks. In 1913 such jobs were all filled and probably had a waiting list; a man thought himself lucky to have regular hours as an overworked stooge; to be a dog's-body was then almost a career.

In that year I began to lead a café life, giving a brief

imitation of a Central European character. I must have found time for it by no longer hurrying to my attic to write *Moorton Sketches* and the like. The café where we spent so much time and so little money was a Lyons in Market Street. It was a long narrow place divided by a short flight of stairs. The solid customers munched away on the ground level; we golden lads, without even a glance around, made straight for the upper level, the back room you might say, where we were capable of monopolising a couple of tables for hours while spending about sixpence a head. Oddly enough, we were not discouraged, at least not by anybody in sight, though distant accountants and general managers cannot have regarded us as promising patrons; indeed, this was a branch that Lyons soon lopped off. The waitresses, all young and mostly from London and Ireland, were on our side, keeping our tables, passing on messages, joining our conspiracy against accountancy and the interests of shareholders. Once a friend and I took two of the prettiest out for a Sunday walk on the moors and a high tea; and mine, Irish, though she still looked pretty enough out of uniform and in the open air, was not the companion she promised to be when on duty, for she never stopped reciting bad verse and sketching scenes from melodramas, a dotty and tedious wench.

In a space to the right, as you arrived at the top of the stairs that separated the poets from the peasants, the trio performed. Even now I can see them quite clearly, these three instrumentalists, when every feature of some important personages has vanished from memory. I cannot imagine why they have stayed with me like archetypal images; I am writing in my sixty-eighth year of this life and understand little or nothing. The violinist was a mop-haired, dark, beaky, flashing-eyed fellow, who might have been a standard romantic fiddler of the period delivered straight from Italy, but was in fact as English as we were. The pianist was a big fattish man, rather like a ruined bishop; detached, mysterious, he seemed to have no interest in music, in Lyons, in us or the waitresses; he may have been silently refuting Hegel or wondering about the Gobi Desert. The 'cellist, whom we knew better than we did the other two, wore his brown hair short and had a clipped moustache; his face, daintily smudged under the eyes, was not unpleasing though it always looked rather crumpled, airless and weary; he suggested somebody between a youngish un-waxed *croupier* and the dissipated secretary of a gold-mining company. It was he whom we teased or bullied out of playing yet again the waltz 'Destiny' or the 'Indian Love Lyrics', and through his good offices the trio occasionally gave us some real music. I cannot hear that music, but I can see again the ghost of a grin haunting the 'cellist's moustache, the look the violinist flashed in our direction, the large indifferent back of the pianist, Schubert and Lionel Monckton all one to him. Perhaps somewhere in their place along the fourth dimension, immortally enduring in the fifth dimension, that trio is still performing at the top of the stairs in Lyons, Market Street, Bradford; and if I were a more sensitive type I could not only see it but hear it.

When we stopped arguing in the café, descending the stairs into the world again, we might be going to look at and listen to those girls, too ladylike for us, who chanted Gilbert Murray's Euripidean choruses for Penelope Wheeler; to frown at the wind machine in Strauss's *Don Quixote*; to take a tram in the direction of certain moorland cottages hiding suffragettes on the run; to help entertain the Irish Players who had come to raise money for Jim Larkin. I was writing verse, perhaps some of the stuff I have already mentioned, and pursuing, not in vain, the girl who played Ann in *Man and Superman* and similar parts in the Playgoers' Society readings. I still assisted the export of crossbred tops to Germany, Sweden and Rhode Island, but in a dream. On several mornings, when the sun was already climbing high and there was not a cloud, I turned my back on the tram to town and went striding the opposite way, playing truant, to walk all day across the moors. We were all great walkers then, with the best walking country in the world so close; before the motor-car had taken possession of England; when what are now motoring roads, bristling with signs and warnings, were still moorland tracks. I knew men who walked forty miles or so every fine Sunday, swinging rather stiffly from the hips, the upper body bent forward a little, in a kind of long lurch that looks ungainly, in a drovers' and shepherds' style, but devours the upland miles unwearyingly, almost without effort until the end of the day. I was one of the indolent, a mere lounger, but even so I thought nothing of twenty miles or more; and later, marching in the Army, never once failed to stay in the column when man after man was dropping out and others were staggering on blindly, unable to shoulder the rifles the remainder of us had to carry for them. And walking over the moors on these days when I played truant, I was, I remember, never happier; my mind was no more overshadowed with guilt than the sky was with cloud; the thought that here I was, alone and free, while others of my kind were at their desks, added brightness and gold to the sunlight, freshness to the air, music to the singing larks; every wandering moorland path, clean as sea sand where I walked and glittering ahead, was delectable, promising everything. Every moment of those truant walks is alive in me still; perhaps I would not be writing now if it were not for them; I am being nourished through a long winter by stolen fruit.

During the first eight months of 1914, one might say, I was running round at a standstill. I was cramming the hours with experience, tasting this and gulping down that, widening my acquaintance, making a few new friends; but in the centre of all this nothing much was happening. My life was like a round-about with the gilded cars and cockerels flashing by, the bray of the organ, the drums and cymbals, never silent, while the man in the middle wipes his hands on an oily rag and yawns. I have never been much of a planner, but at this time I was not visited by even the ghost of a plan. Not only did I not know which way I was going, I never even looked to see if there were any signposts, any paths. I had not the least notion what I was going to do, and now – or so it seems, if memory is not cheating – at last nobody, not even my father, asked me. Afterwards, thinking back to this time, I asked myself questions to which there could be no answers. What had happened to my idea of a-pound-a-week-in-a-cottage? When did I think I could put my name to a book? If I refused to consider any move, how much longer did I think I could stay where I was? And indeed how much longer could the office and I tolerate each other? What did I think I was doing anyhow, in this spring and summer of 1914? But the self that survived the War, putting such questions almost angrily, twenty-five-year-old to nineteen-year-old, could not supply the answers himself; and he was out of touch with that Bradford youth; the canyon smoking between them was too wide, too deep, also too new. Now, so far removed that twenty-five and nineteen seem to be joined, the gap bridged, I can bring to each question the same answer: I believe I know now what was happening that summer. I believe I did nothing but enjoy what could be enjoyed because we were soon to be at war. Con-sciously of course we never entertained a thought of it; but deep in the unconscious, which has its own time and a wider *now* than consciousness knows, already the war was on, a world ending.

Again, I chose June for my fortnight's holiday, 'wangling' –

a term I did not know then, but it was rushing to meet me – another free pass, this time from Hull to Holland. I stayed in Amsterdam a day or two, staring at the Rembrandts and Vermeers. My luggage on my back, I set out from Cologne on a walking tour of the Rhine, not the river I have often seen since but another one, lost, gone. I bought and smoked one of those yard-long pipes, still in common use then, not manufactured for the tourist trade; I stayed in tiny inns, buried among leaves, swimming in green air; I strummed on pianos in low-ceilinged back rooms for peasant tenors and basses who put down pipes even larger than mine, calling for more rounds of wine and beer. I had a roaring good time, not in this world, perhaps not even in that other which was ending; I suspect now I was having a walking tour in picaresque and romantic literature. I came back by way of Belgium, staying in Brussels for one-franc-fifty in a rather sinister decaying hotel, where I slept uneasily in that enormous bed, itself uneasy on the creaking floor, which looms in so many old travellers' tales, Uppsala to Granada. The city itself, though, was still leafy and comparatively small then, an operetta kind of capital, where I could exchange the few gold coins I had left for superb food and drink, and where, most suitably, I saw and heard for the first time *Der Rosenkavalier*. When I sailed for Hull, late at night, late in June, later still in an epoch, I watched the lights of Europe retreat to a glimmer and then vanish from my sight for ever. I ought to have heard a vast muted orchestra and *Ewig, ewig* – but I knew no Mahler then. Those lights, that shore, really were gone for ever. The Europe I left that night sank into history, banishing itself from immediate experience as my Atlantis had done when the sea sucked it down.

In August 1914, when the newsboys were running and shouting every day and all day, I was alone in the house, my family being at the seaside. I waited until they came back before I enlisted, in early September. Years later, I often asked myself why I had joined the Army. The usual explanations were no good. I was not hot with patriotic feeling; I did not believe that Britain was in any real danger. I was sorry for 'gallant little Belgium' but did not feel she was waiting for me to rescue her. The legend of Kitchener, who pointed at us from every hoarding, had never captured me. I was not under any pressure from public opinion, which had not got to work on young men as early as that; the white feathers came later. I was not carried to the recruiting office in a herd rush of chums, nobody thinking, everybody half-plastered; I went alone. (Most of my friends joined elsewhere and later, when the local 'Pals' Battalion' was formed – and in July 1916, on the Somme, that battalion might have been dry moorland grass to which somebody put a match.) I was not simply swapping jobs; though the office bored me, life in the Army certainly did not attract me, and for some years I had regarded with contempt those lads who wanted to wear a uniform and be marched about. This was no escape to freedom and independence; I may not have known much about military life, but I was not so green. And I certainly did not see myself as a hero, whose true stature would be revealed by war; that had never been one of my illusions. What is left then to supply a motive?

Nothing, I believe now, that was rational and conscious. Remember that for months before, as I have already suggested, though enjoying myself, perhaps almost feverishly, I had come to a standstill, refusing to make any plan, even to consider the future, really because in that other time scale of the unconscious my world had already ended. I was kept from making any move by some mysterious prompting from the dark of my mind. And now, prompted again, there was a move I had to make. I went at a signal from the unknown. In my enlistment there was more than a hint of another in Shake-speare, no clattering King Harry stuff, no baronial banging about, but that scene in which Feeble, the women's tailor, is pricked by Justice Shallow to serve Sir John Falstaff. (Not, vanity insists, that I resembled Feeble outwardly, being a strongly-built and well-exercised youth.) It was Feeble, whose name Shakespeare should have changed after he turned him from a walk-on into a character, who replied to Falstaff's first jeering challenge: 'I will do my good will, sir; you can have no more.' And then later, when he knows he will have to go, he observes immortally, this badly-named Feeble: 'By my troth, I care not; a man can die but once; we owe God a death: I'll ne'er bear a base mind.' At first sight this passive acceptance, this shrugging fatalism of the conscript, may seem too far away from our quick and indeed eager volunteering. I do not think so. There came, out of the unclouded blue of that summer, a challenge that was almost like a conscription of the spirit, little to do really with King and Country and flag-waving and hip-hip-hurrah, a challenge to what we felt was our untested manhood. Other men, who had not lived as easily as we had, had drilled and marched and borne arms – couldn't we? Yes, we too could leave home and soft beds and the girls to soldier for a spell, if there was some excuse for it, something at least to be defended. And here it was.

All this applies only to those early weeks and that 'First Hundred Thousand'. War might drive a man till he dropped; it could be a dangerous and bloody business; we believed, however, that it still offered movement, colour, adventure, and drama. Later, when the murderous idiotic machinery of the Western Front was grinding away, of course all was different; then we knew better what kind of game this was. But what I had felt at first, the idea of not refusing a challenge, a test like some tribe's initiation into manhood, lingered on, as I have discovered from reading one or two of the earliest letters I wrote home from the front line, in the summer of 1915. The old box-file mentioned before, containing the notebooks and manuscripts, showed me these letters. They are not explicit, but the idea is there, though, peeping out between the astonishingly matter-of-fact lines. If I had needed a clue to my state of mind when I enlisted, it was here, inside one of these old green Active Service envelopes. That I did not need it is further proof that what I remember best, at this distance from youth, are its states of mind.

So early in September I joined, like a chump, the infantry – to be precise, the Duke of Wellington's West Riding Regiment, known in some circles as 'The Havercake Lads', in others as 'The Dirty Duke's'. I hurried along Market Street, a Swan Arcadian late again, for the last time. Instead of asking the boss if there was anything more, I shook his outstretched hand, then walked out of junior clerkdom for ever. I reported at the regimental depot in Halifax, where a regular sergeant, noting sardonically the newish sports coat and flannel trousers that, like a fool, I was wearing, set me to work at once removing the congealed fat from immense cooking pots. For a week or so I was free to return home at night, so long as I was back in barracks before eight in the morning. Now through all this time that was ending, the great double-decked electric tram, already often mentioned but never celebrated, had gone groaning and stopping and starting again, 'the high-built glittering galleon of the streets'; maddening of course yet more than indispensable, a kind of clumsy comrade, hardly our horse, perhaps our immense camel, our illuminated elephant. It took us to and from work, drama and music, encounters with girls; it could turn our faces to the moors, untarnished heights and clean air. Now the last regular tram-rides I ever made – it is the last clear memory I have of this time – were those early morning journeys back to barracks, when I sat yawning and shivering a little, my new Army boots weighing a ton, on the empty tram top as it climbed and groaned up to Queensbury, on the Pennine roof and cold already, and then dropped me among the thickets of mill chimneys in Halifax. I can still put myself on that tram, still feel those boots and the puttees that were too tight or too slack; though I have forgotten most of what happened at the end of the ride. I think I tried to walk smartly, though I was still more of a Swan Arcadian than a soldier, past the guard at the barracks entrance. And what I do know for certain is that that entrance was up Gibbet Lane. From Hull, Hell and Halifax, our great-grandfathers declared, God must defend us. I had sailed to Hull from a Europe I never knew again. I had arrived at Halifax to begin my soldiering. Hell, no doubt, was on its way.

PART TWO

Carry On, Carry On!
(1914-1919)

From early September 1914 until the middle of March 1919, I was in the Army. I enlisted in my twentieth year and was demobilised in my twenty-fifth. Now it is true, as I have already declared, that I am not attempting an autobiography here, simply an account of my writing life. It is also true that during these four-and-a-half years in the Army I did very little writing. With these facts in mind, I did not intend at first to describe these years. But the gap is too wide to be jumped; the whole of my earlier twenties cannot be ignored; and I do not think my professional life and work, which arrive in the next section, can be understood without some account of these years of soldiering. This does not mean I propose to dig World War One out of the clay and chalk and rotting sandbags where I found it. An impressive amount of first-hand reporting – some of it, by my contemporaries, very fine indeed – already exists; and anything new about that war must be said by much younger men, who are already beginning to tell us how it looks to them as history. The best I can do here is to bridge the gap between 1914 and 1919, and at the same time to suggest what contribution these war years may have made to my writing life. Any direct contribution will be very small; the indirect one, on levels out of reach of a good memory and any desire to be truthful and candid, may have been enormous; but obviously I can discover only a part of it here. That is why, with little or no writing to refer to, I treat this as a bridge passage. And of course I am the subject, not the war.

The time factor is curious. When I look back on my life, seeing it as a road I have travelled, these four-and-a-half years shrink at once; they seem nothing more than a queer bend in the road full of dust and confusion. But when memory really goes to work and I re-enter those years, then just because they used up all my earlier twenties (I was actually in the front-line trenches for my twenty-first birthday) they suddenly turn into a whole epoch, almost another life in another world. I can well believe that younger men and women feel much the same about the Second War. But I think the First War cut deeper and played more tricks with time because it *was* first, because it was bloodier, because it came out of a blue that nobody saw after 1914. The map that came to pieces in 1939 was never the apparently solid arrangement that blew up in 1914. Any intelligent European born, let us say, after 1904 reached the teens in what he or she knew to be a dangerous and cruel world. But if you were born in 1894, as I was, you suddenly saw a great jagged crack in the looking-glass. After that your mind could not escape from the idea of a world that ended in 1914 and another one that began about 1919, with a wilderness of smoke and fury, outside sensible time, lying between them. Any reader of my *Literature and Western Man* will remember that I am very emphatic there about this division, the ending of one age and the beginning of another. I am not apologising for this emphasis – there are plenty of good impersonal reasons for it – but I am sure I could never honestly avoid it : I left one world to spend an exile in limbo, came out of it to find myself in another world.

I have read the wartime letters home that have survived; I have looked at a map or two just because I am often vague about places; but what is far more important is that I have tried to return along the road to that queer bend, plunged into that dust and confusion, time expanding as memory goes to work, to discover states of mind that remain when the order of events, together with all military life, is a jumble and half a dream. This places me immediately in one of the two classes

[88]

into which writers and artists who served in that war can be divided. There are those – and Hemingway may stand for many writers – who found in war, however much they hated it, the deeper reality we all look for. From those depths, a cold bubbling spring, came their inspiration. I remember dining for the first and last time, many years ago, with a fellow Yorkshireman, C. S. Jagger the sculptor. I liked him but did not much care for most of the work of his that I had seen. But that night he showed me a low relief of no man's land, amazingly skilful, pulling distances out of quarter inches, that had for me great emotional force. The war, burning in memory, had set the craftsman on fire and transformed him into an artist. And almost all these men, like Jagger, like Hemingway for all his immense prestige, seemed to feel more confused and unhappy as the war receded, as if they felt they were drifting away from reality, as if a world with its guns silent was an uneasy dream. To this class, neither inferior nor superior but different, I never belonged. The dream began for me when the guns roared. Except at certain rare moments, and these were far outnumbered by their peacetime counterparts, I did not discover any deeper reality in war. I never hailed with relief, as men in the opposing class did, a wholly masculine way of life uncomplicated by Woman. Its obvious one-sidedness soon made it seem to me a vast piece of imbecility. However hard-pressed, even desperate, I may have been at times in the years after the war, never for one moment did I long to be back in the Army. Now and then I remember with some nostalgia the England of the Second World War, when my nation had a bright image of itself and the rat-race was not yet on; but never those four-and-a-half years of the First War. Anybody searching these pages for the spirit of the regimental dinner and the reunion will be disappointed. Everybody else may be disappointed too; but that I cannot help.

2

After a week or two going by early morning tram from home
to the barracks in Halifax, I left with a thousand others, by
train at four in the morning, for a tented camp at Frensham in
Surrey. There I found myself in Number 8 Platoon, B Company, 10th Duke of Wellington's, 69th Brigade, 23rd Division.
Until the rains of winter finally washed us out of this camp
altogether, we slept twelve in a bell-tent, kneeling after
Lights Out to piss in our boots and then emptying them under
the flap. The old soldiers told us that this was good for our
boots, making them easier for route marches. Unlike battalions
formed later, we had plenty of old soldiers, many of whom had
served in India and carried little tins of curry powder to
sprinkle over any meat that came their way. Some of them of
course were already wearing crowns or stripes, but many
others, dour or wily types, refused promotion. They would do
what they considered their essential duty, and in all circumstances as time proved, but they were, so to speak, against the
military Establishment, would not be associated with it, and
remained suspicious and grumbling privates to the end.
(Though genuinely anxious, during the first year or so, to get
into some fighting, I soon discovered that I belonged by
temperament to this type myself.) We were almost all West
Riding men. In my company there were a few suburban junior
clerks and the like, of my sort, with whom I soon made friends.
And the closer of these, those whose names I still remember,
were all killed, even before the Somme battles in 1916. Most
of the others were mill workers of various kinds. In my own
platoon, by an odd chance, were some men, with names like
Grady, Murphy, O'Neill, who came from the local 'back o't

mill' where my mother, whose name was Hoult, had grown
up: they were almost cousins of mine. Perhaps it was the Irish
in them that lifted their grumbling, which never stopped, to an
Elizabethan height. The only remarks I have ever heard that
Shakespeare might have borrowed all came from private
soldiers in that war.

It is not true, as some young critics of the First War British
high command have suggested, that Kitchener's Army consisted of brave but half-trained amateurs, so much pitiful
cannon fodder. In the earlier divisions like ours, the troops had
months and months of severe intensive training. Our average
programme was ten hours a day, and nobody grumbled more
than the old regulars, who had never been compelled before to
do so much for so long. It was only in musketry that we were
far behind the Regular Army, simply because we had to wait
for months for the rifles we would eventually use. We began
without any equipment at all. There was not enough khaki
cloth for regulation uniforms, and I remember my own
mortification – I had been one of the few who were wearing
khaki a day after enlistment – when I had to turn in my
uniform and wear instead a doleful convict-style blue outfit,
together with a ridiculous little forage cap and a civilian overcoat. We never felt ourselves to be soldiers again, hardly
wanted to go out, until, as excited as girls, we tore off that
dismal blue, somebody's bad idea, and put on real khaki
uniforms. When we stood for hours in rain and sleet, waiting
to be inspected by Kitchener and Millerand, the blue dye ran
out of our forage caps; I do not know if we looked like clowns
or murderous Indian braves; we felt like both. For my
Christmas leave, I remember that somewhere or other I
picked up an old, much larger and dead-black forage cap,
which gave me – or so I fancied – a half-raffish, half-sinister
look; and when I wore this and a long black overcoat, part of a

swap, and the oddest of the scarves I had been sent, I looked a long way from Kitchener's Army, somebody who had enlisted in some dark bloodthirsty legion in Tashkent; or so, forgetting my innocent pudding face and guileless Bradford accent, I hoped. Certainly the girls I knew at home stared at me in bewilderment lit with fascination: 'Ah knew you'd joined up, Jack – but – Ah mean to say – what are you *in*?'

The only time off we had at Frensham was Sunday afternoon and early evening, and two or three of us, to get out of the camp, would walk to various farmhouses where we could eat a huge sixpenny tea and then, a rare pleasure, sit in front of a fire. It is odd to remember now how rural and remote that Surrey countryside seemed in 1914: the farmhouses, their enormous kitchen fireplaces hung with hams, looked in my eyes then to be out of Thomas Hardy. It was not until late November, after the whole camp had been sinking into mud for weeks, that we were finally washed out of Frensham. I had come to loathe those dripping and steaming bell-tents. Some objects are to my mind symbols of that half of England I detest, and one of them, mean and cramping and a miserable idea, is the bell-tent. Aldershot, where we moved into barracks at last, was no Victorian inspiration. a whole town given up to button-polishing and saluting, bugle calls and guards turning out; but after Frensham its brick huts were a Ritz. It was from Aldershot, some weeks later, towards the end of February 1915, that we made what I call in my jubilant letter home 'the great march', ending for our battalion at Folkestone. We went a roundabout way; only towns of some size could provide the schools and public halls where we slept; we averaged twenty miles a day for several days, and on one day marched over twenty-six miles, not bad going when you remember the weight of full equipment we had to carry then, and that we were moving (I take this out of my letter) in a column a mile and a quarter long. We looked like soldiers now; all four battalions had a band; and all along the route we were waved at and cheered, not foolishly either, for an infantry brigade marching in full equipment with its bands booming and clashing is an impressive spectacle. This was my idea of soldiering – constant movement, unknown destinations, fluttering handkerchiefs and cheers – and I enjoyed it hugely, sore feet and bully-beef and kips on hard floors and all.

Without being told in advance and, as I said in a letter 'five miles from anywhere', we were inspected by Kitchener. This time I had a close view, finding him older and greyer than the familiar pictures of him. The image I retained was of a rather bloated purplish face and glaring but somehow jellied eyes, an image not of an ageing man, already bewildered by, reeling under, the load of responsibility he refused to share, but of some larger-than-life yet now less-than-life figure, huge but turning into painted lead. It was a frightening and not pleasing image, and a year later, when we heard he had been drowned, I felt no grief, for it did not seem to me that a man had lost his life: I saw only a heavy shape, its face now an idol's, going down and down into that northern sea. Yet it was he – and he alone – who had raised us new soldiers out of the ground. This, not anything he did in Egypt and the Sudan and India, was a stroke of genius; he created armies when all the others, mischievous clowns like Henry Wilson or the huntin'-and-shootin' cavalry captains pretending to be generals, said he was an obstinate old fool and laughed at him. Here I was, I still am, on his side. But the image that remained after that inspection, of something immensely massive and formidable but already hardening and petrifying, nearer to death than to life, haunted me to my disquiet for a long time. Even when at last we reeled through a cleft in the Downs, saw the sea and gave a cheer, straightened our shoulders for the final miles along the clean and twinkling edge of it, swinging through Hythe and Sandgate, that image was there, the eyes glaring out of death not life.

In Folkestone we were billeted in private houses. On my arrival I wrote home gleefully to announce this, saying I would sleep in a bed and have real meals, like having a holiday at the seaside. But of course I added this holiday bit to cheer them up at home. Actually at this time, bored with drill and exercises, physical and military, I began to look out for odd jobs that would keep me off parade. Earlier I had refused to become an orderly-room clerk; I had not joined the Army to exchange one office for another. On the other hand, though not lazy, still with energy to burn, I now found the sheer repetitiveness of parades and exercises hard to endure. Moreover, most of us felt it was time we were sent out to the Front, now that we had had seven months' hard training. Indeed, three of us decided that if the battalion were still in England in eight or ten weeks – I forget the date we agreed upon – then we would desert, to join up again at some depot where men were being sent out almost at once. This could happen even early in 1915; if a regular battalion had been heavily punished in the line and there was a shortage of regular reserves at the depot, then some recruits might be drafted to the Front. This explains why some untrained men did find themselves in the trenches even then; but of course it does not justify the statement that whole New Army divisions had had no proper training and were a kind of brave rabble. Meanwhile, at Folkestone I was rescued from boredom by being sent, with another man, to do 'officers' mess fatigue' for the duration of our stay there.

This was not a cushy job in terms of work and hours, but I enjoyed it. We were washers-up and kitchen dog's-bodies. The Mess, in a detached villa, was being run by a catering firm

– I think, though I could not swear to it, the Junior Army and Navy Stores. The staff were all civilians. The chef was a Frenchman, fattish and untidy, always angry because the kitchen range was inadequate for his needs and he had to perform miracles of improvisation and sharp timing. I never saw him sit down to a meal; he drank a good deal and nearly always had a ragged cigarette smouldering and drooping; he would droop and smoulder too, then go blazing into action. The waiters were middle-aged professionals with a code and jargon all their own. One of them, melancholy, blue-chinned, with those beaten spaniel's eyes that seem to encourage women to misbehave, was having trouble with his wife, who was unfaithful and might leave him for ever at any moment; and she kept rushing in to make a scene and provide drama that we all enjoyed. The wine waiter, a suave young man beautifully dressed, had been the valet of a well-known aristocratic type, who afterwards became even better-known and must be nameless here. Milord had gone to the front, but this valet could not follow him because he had been rejected on medical grounds; so here he was. When neither of us was busy he told me stories of dissolute high life as strange and fascinating to me as passages from the *Arabian Nights*; one of them, describing how milord and his mistress used anchovy paste in their sexual play, makes me marvel even now. My fatigue mate, a dour man from Huddersfield who smoked thick twist in a short curved pipe, just did what he had to do, devoured the excellent food we were given, lit his pipe and vanished; but I loved to explore and savour this backstairs world so new to me, this behind-the-scenes of catering, and so did not resent the long hours, which left me just sufficient time to smoke a pipe or two on the Leas in the late morning, when the band played, and to take a walk after the lunch dishes, an immense pile, had been washed, dried, cleared, and before the evening chores began.

To this day, if need be, I can wash up and dry as fast as anybody I know; but other skills I learnt then – for example, I could toast eight slices of bread at the same time, using four toasting-forks – have decayed for lack of use. We lived well in the kitchen, the staff looking after its own; many a time I saw a fine portion of some specially good dish set aside for me when I could hear in the distance the waiters telling belated officers in the dining-room that that dish was 'off'. A writer of my sort is a man who likes to get behind the scenes. Already I was in training.

I found myself behind very different scenes when we left Folkestone for Maidstone, where the battalion was sent to dig trenches for the outer ring of London's defences, and where on the first night we all got drunk on the uncommonly strong local ale. I detested digging, in which the few navvies among us made us all look silly by setting to work slowly and methodically and shifting about three times as much soil as we did; so I was delighted when I was given a stripe and put in charge of the company's billeting arrangements. Each house-holder was paid a fixed sum per day – let us say, as a near guess, 3s. 7½d. – for providing board and lodging. I had to allot these billets, for which the supply far exceeded the demand, pay for them, and deal with complaints from either side. It was tricky, and I learnt much about the private life of Maidstone. Some of the senior N.C.O.s wanted to change their billets not neces-sarily because of any lack of food and comfort but because they were lured away by housewives more comely, amiable and compliant than others. I myself changed my billet, after the second day, because an extremely pretty girl called Dorothy, a cool and sharp wench, sought me out to tell me that her mother, a widow, had room for one soldier and couldn't I send them one, please, *please*? So I sent them myself. They seemed to be a family that had come down in the world, living sparely in a ramshackle house; the whole set-up was like a play, though not the kind of play that was being produced in 1915. There was this sharp and bright-eyed Dorothy, who really ran the show although she was only about eighteen and who, unless she had the worst of luck, probably restored the family fortunes later; there was her rather bewildered, defeated and gentle mother; and sleeping among the lumber in the attic was a kind of vague gnome, with a suggestion of the holy fool about him, called Tommy, who was no relation but earned enough to give them a few shillings a week. Nor was that all, for Dorothy's older sister was a film actress – a fantastic profession then – and once when she was filming not too far away she came dashing home, astonishing me by her mask of yellow make-up, her chain-smoking, her drinks and nervous uninhibited talk. She seemed to me as exotic, as remote from any young woman I had ever seen before, as a mandarin's concubine.

It never occurred to me that I would at any time penetrate into the mysterious world she represented. But I had already felt something like this – even though they did not look as strange as Dorothy's sister, and I was not observing them so closely – about several actresses who had come to entertain us earlier. The one I remember best, from a Sunday night show at Frensham given by some musical-comedy players, was Nellie Taylor, a favourite at that time. I have just looked her up to discover that, after having left the stage for some years, she was only thirty-eight when she died in 1932. This means that she was exactly my age, so that she can have been no more than twenty when I stared at her, that Sunday night in 1914, over the rows of officers' smooth heads. It was not any particular talent she showed that excited me then and made me remember her; now in fact I cannot recall what she did. No, it was the way she looked and sounded, her undisguised enjoyment of the

situation in which she found herself that night, the dancing
light of her high spirits, her quintessential young femininity,
to which my heart went out. All this brought me joy in this
vast snarling clutter of men; but mixed with this joy was a
painful feeling of being altogether outside her world, not
Shaftesbury Avenue and the Savoy Grill but some shining
mysterious region of unattainable girls. I felt a sense of exile
and loss, a wound that still ached long after that evening. When
she blew us her last kisses and vanished, the lights went down
for weeks, my Army boots felt heavier and clumsier than ever.

In high summer – it seemed hot that year – we left for what
was really a new wooden town, hutments for all the division,
at Bramshott in Hampshire. Now we no longer talked of
deserting to get to the Front; every day brought rumours,
usually picked up in the latrines, about where and when we
should be going. In the cool of the evening my friends and I
would solemnly discuss these rumours as we walked, rather
stiffly, the two miles or so to Haslemere. But that was before
something, I have forgotten what, happened to the battalion
post corporal, and I was commanded to take over his duties,
which left me little leisure and no social life at all. I was now
identified with missing letters, parcels that ought to have
turned up a week before; all ranks stopped me and eyed me
suspiciously – 'Now, look here, are you sure there was nothing
for me today? Because if so there's something bloody queer
going on'; I was no longer a man and a brother. Our old
colonel, too old for service at the front, had watched us march
past for the last time, not hiding his tears, suddenly ancient
and done with now. We had a new C.O., who had been a
Regular Army major and who spoke with what seemed to my
ears such a fantastically affected drawl, I could not take him
seriously; he was like a comic swell in a play. I was released
from those damnable letters and parcels, slept in some

imitation trenches and did some bomb-throwing, enjoyed a night or two of bivouacking because the dust and heat of the camp became intolerable and the tar on the hut roofs was melting and dripping through. Then after a brief last leave, spent mostly in crowded trains which as they moved along the platforms, as if pulling a horrible string, jerked away smiles and then crumpled so many women's faces, we waited about until it was very late and dark one night, and sailed for France.

3

In France I was hotter than I had ever been in my life before, just as in a few months' time I was to be wetter and colder. Humping along those cobbled roads in full marching order, choked by the dust of military transport, was murderous, and even the rat-infested barns we slept in every night never seemed to have known cool fresh air. Yet while aware of un-pleasant physical sensations, I felt at heart detached from them, moving – as I wrote in my first letter home – almost floating, in a long dream. I suspect that this feeling, that here was no reality, never from this time entirely left me, out at the Front or back at home, until the day I was demobilised, nearly four years later. Unlike some later divisions, who found them-selves entangled in German barbed wire and slaughtered by machine-gun fire before they knew where they were, we were lucky, being initiated by degrees. We relieved the long-service Regulars of the 8th Division in what was then a quiet sector, Bois Grenier – Laventie – Fleurbaix, where in many places the two front lines were wide apart, so that we had listening posts out in no man's land. I spent two or three hours alone in one of these, I think on my second or third night in the line, staring so hard at black nothing that it stopped being black or nothing and began to crawl with greyish shapes; I would then shut my eyes for a few moments, and when I opened them again the shapes had vanished. I do not think I am flattering my twenty-year-old self if I say that I was less apprehensive in that listening post than I am now on all manner of comparatively safe occasions. Youth, hard training, a genuine desire to get *into* the war at some point, had turned me temporarily into a brave soldier. I was less and less brave, in that sense, the more and more I saw of this war. The truth is, as anybody can discover from the behaviour of very young children, terror arrives first through the ear. Turn off the sound on a television set, when old newsreels of war, later of course than the 1914–18 War, are on the screen, and the menace goes; we stare unmoved at a shadow play. Turn the sound on again, even though it has been cut down and muffled, and the scenes are alive and terrible again. Now the First War, with its massed artillery, was the noisiest of all time; the sound hit you harder and harder as the months passed; some things you got used to – sniping and machine-gun fire if you were not entangled in the open and a sitting duck, hand-bombs and rifle grenades if you had sandbags and room to dodge – but as time went on the vast cannonading, drumming hell into your ears, no matter whether it was their guns or yours, began to wear you down, making you feel that flesh and blood had no place in this factory of destruction. So in that war it was not the recruit but the veteran who began to feel he was being hammered into the ground. Every time I went back into the line, especially after being out of it long enough for my ears to be open to civilisation again, I felt more and more apprehension. In that listening post I was the gallant Tommy of the home-front legends; but as time wore on I was more and more a chap who wondered what the hell he was doing there and how the hell he could get out of it – a mouse in a giant mincing machine.

In that sector, where in places we were not in real trenches at all but between breastworks of sandbags, there were still, of all things, catapults here and there, big ones, the kind the Romans had used. We were in fact still short of guns and ammunition. But when we moved over to the right, nearer Neuve Chapelle, we knew that guns and ammunition were piling up behind us. On the 25th September 1915, when the disastrous Battle of Loos was fought, we were in the front line, wearing full kit and so weighed down with extra cartridges and bombs we could hardly move, waiting to climb the scaling ladders all along the fire trench. Over our heads, where the ladders would take us, invisible express trains seemed to be passing both ways, there was such an unceasing exchange of shells. Once up the ladders and out of the trench, I felt a cat would not live five minutes. But the luck was in – I had a lucky war – and because the attack on our right had not gained sufficient ground we were never thrown into the assault, stayed where we were, and saw the scaling ladders taken away. In the months that followed, after the rains came, then sleet and snow, there were no more full-scale attacks, only occasional raids. These could be very unpleasant, and I was on one when the barbed wire entanglements, which the artillery said had been cut there, proved to be still intact; and there we were, trapped, no longer in darkness but in the sinister illumination of star shells and pistol lights, asking to be machine-gunned out of this world, as many were. I never knew how many, but I know that another man and I, untouched, somehow contrived to crawl back, half-carrying and half-dragging between us a third man, badly wounded.

Worse then than the raids, worse than the German heavy batteries that occasionally got our range and dropped 'Jack Johnsons' among us, were the mere conditions of existence in the front line and communication trenches, now with winter upon

us, that were mud and water. For days and days on end, wearing six pairs of socks and high gum-boots and a sheepskin
jacket that was either wet or caked in mud, I slithered around,
trying to sleep on the trench firestep or crawling into some
hole in the wet clay, filthy and maddeningly lousy, never seeing
anything that looked like hot food. (I was fortunate, more than
most, in two respects: I could cheerfully chew away at Army
biscuits and bully-beef, which was all we had many days; I was
rarely out of tobacco, and if I could smoke my pipe I could often
forget I was hungry and short of sleep.) That dugout we have
all seen in productions of *Journey's End* would have looked to
me then like a suite in some Grand Hotel: I never did find
myself within miles of anything so dry and commodious. Some
of the worst nights, in that winter of 1915, were spent carrying
heavy coils of barbed wire up communication trenches, knee-
deep in water and sometimes under shellfire, continually
slipping and then being pinned down by the coils of wire. I
saw men, no weaklings but powerful fellows, break down and
weep. It was not the danger, which might easily have been
worse – though at that I lost every close friend I had in the
company that winter – but the conditions in which the lower
ranks of the infantry were condemned to exist month after
month, worse conditions than the Germans and French ever
knew except briefly in battle, that drained away health,
energy, spirit, and with them any real confidence in those
cavalry captains, back in the châteaux, who saw themselves as
generals fit for high command. They tell me Passchendaele in
'17 was worse still – I was never there, thank God – and now I
believe the Army ought to have turned on Haig and his friends
and sent them home. Even without the negotiated peace we
ought to have had in 1916, we could have saved half a million
British lives if we had handed the whole mess over to a few
men from Imperial Chemicals, Lever Brothers or Lyons and Co.

Sometimes we were in situations impossible to imagine, far stranger than bad dreams. I wonder how many men still alive remember being in that support trench that ran through a French village cemetery. There we had great crosses and monuments of marble and granite all round us, unbelievable at night when the darkness was split by the white glare of Véry lights and the shadows were gigantically grotesque, though often we had not time to notice them, having to duck down as machine-gun bullets ricocheted off the funeral stones. I cannot remember now whether it was before or after I knew this Edgar Allan Poe setting that I was whisked away for a week or so to do some clerking at Third Corps headquarters, taking the place of a man who had gone to hospital. We worked and slept in a wooden hut, receiving, decoding, distributing or filing telegrams, starting fairly early in the morning and finishing between ten and eleven at night. The only break I had was during the afternoon, when I would walk in the grounds of the château with a little London clerk, who had a wife and children and dreaded any possibility of going up into the line. We had little to say to each other on these melancholy walks; the château grounds were almost without colour and form, deep in wintry weather that had no ice and glitter; we were like two empty sad characters in one of those *avant-garde* films or novels in which nothing happens. Though safe and dry for once, I hated this job and this place, and longed to get back to the men I knew, trenches and shellfire and all. The staff warrant officer in charge of us was one of those sadistic types often found far behind the line; he bullied and tormented men like my London acquaintance who were in terror of being sent into action; there was a smell of fear in that hut; and he disliked me from the first, and after he threatened to return me to my battalion and I told him that was what I wanted, nothing I did was right.

It was like being a low-grade civil servant, working double shifts, being sworn at all the time, not getting enough to eat, and still feeling dirty and lice-itchy. And all the telegrams, many of them unnecessary and making no sense, all the filing and fuss, together created a Kafka atmosphere, though of course it was years before I found this name for it. But after that hut, trapped in the middle of what seemed a huge idiotic system, I have never rid myself of the feeling that we British – perhaps the whole Western world – both in war and peace are now committed to wasting men and time and money collecting and receiving and distributing and filing unnecessary information, and that before we go broke and barmy we should hire a team of bold haters of clerical work to cut nine-tenths of it out. Let them empty floor after floor of those ministerial buildings, rising higher every year, burn or pulp those acres of filing systems, cart away tons of in-trays and out-trays, then start again, without Kafka.

After a few more weeks in the line I was wounded in the hand by a rifle grenade, no great matter, not the 'blighty' that sent you to England. I was dispatched to a hospital and then a convalescent camp at Le Tréport on the coast. I did not like either of them, especially the convalescent camp, where we never had enough to eat, were always being rounded up for fatigue duties (detested by all front-line soldiers), and, being cut off, had no money, no letters, no parcels, no anything. I was glad to get back to the battalion, a kind of home, however dangerous and uncomfortable. I was not the keen, fit warrior I had been months before, but I still felt that if I had to wear a uniform, obey orders, serve in France, then I wanted to be with the battalion wherever it was. By this time I might have had a commission but I refused to apply; I still wanted to be with the men who had gone up Gibbet Lane, Halifax, when I did, even though one friend after another was vanishing. Later I was sorry I had not applied; it was a rough war for junior officers but an even rougher one for men in the ranks. It is true that in attack the subalterns had to move around more than their men, and so were more likely to get killed or wounded, but they were not so badgered and sworn at, underfed and overworked, and escaped the very worst conditions. They were all right, our own junior officers; my quarrel, which still continues, was with their superiors, especially the red-tabbed kind, who seemed to me then, so far as I could judge in my raw youth and innocence, mostly a lot of jackasses. And now I am no longer young and have lost all innocence, I see it was a good guess.

In March 1916 the whole division came out of the line, preparing to move further down, to relieve the 17th French Division on the Carency–Souchez front. It happened that I was one of a tiny advance party. A glance at the map today suggests we made the kind of move that would take about forty minutes in a car. But in this war, in another world, another time, it seemed an immense and complicated journey, like going to Afghanistan now. (Much later, it took me three days, never at any point abandoning the journey, to move some men from Rouen to Calais.) We might have been explorers creeping into some blank space on the map. I remember how four or five of us in this advance party, now utterly lost (we had a genius for getting lost) and completely out of touch with the British Expeditionary Force, found ourselves in some unknown French town with nobody to report to, no food, no money to buy any food, so that to bring ourselves out of destitution we had to sell – we called it 'flog' – all but the most essential parts of our kit and equipment. When finally we reached the French lines we made some discoveries that heightened our prejudice against the British higher command. The *poilu*, a bloke supposedly so low in morale that he was near mutiny, enjoyed substantial and tasty hot meals where we would have been opening another tin of bully. Unshaven, untidy and at ease, he sat in deep dugouts passing the wine and talking about women when we would have been – and shortly would be – shoved into forward fire trenches, however bad they were, and then ordered on a raid or given some hopeless task just because it was assumed by château types that muck, jeopardy and misery were good for us. 'I have no hesitation in saying,' I wrote to my father, almost as if I had been sent out to do a report for the Bradford Education Committee, 'that the French soldiers are better fed and better treated than we are – and the British public can put that in their pipe and smoke it!'

These same French now taking it easy were, however, a remnant of the divisions that had stormed these ridges, from Lorette to Vimy, in 1915. The Germans had dug themselves in on the higher ground, from which their artillery, heavy and closely massed, dominated the valuable industrial region still held by the French, who were working coal-pits not ten miles in some places from the front line. This was a very sinister sector into which we crept now, half-blinded by the last snow-storms of the winter. Names there enjoyed a grim notoriety – Notre Dame de Lorette, Souchez, Vimy Ridge, and the Labyrinth. Into the Labyrinth we went, relieving *poilus* who obviously looked relieved. These were old trenches that had simply been wired off, and when we explored them we found them filled with bloodstained clothing, abandoned equipment, heads, legs and arms. Further on, in a trench still open, several of us late at night, bitterly cold, crawled into the nearest dug-out, and soon went to sleep although the straw in there hardly protected us from some uncomfortable objects: in the morning we left that dugout in a hurry, for we had been sleeping with enormous aerial torpedoes. Gone were any communication trenches labelled with the names of London streets; there were no clearly marked fire and support trenches; you crawled through the dark and a belated blizzard and found a hole somewhere. It had been quiet recently around there until we British arrived, but of course we had to hot it up for the sake of our morale, to keep our fellas on their toes, in spite of the fact, not hard to discover on the map and all too obvious to any staff officer who went to see for himself, that if we did start anything the Germans, higher up, well dug in, and in places not more than twenty yards away, would have the better of it. So very soon, having asked for it, God knows why, we caught a packet. Outside any plan of campaign, without any battle being fought, any honours being won, we went through the mincer. It was not long before our own B Company, with a nominal fighting strength of 270, had been reduced to a grim and weary seventy. Two hundred men had gone somehow and somewhere, with nothing to show for it.

Spring came suddenly, and between the pounded and bloody chalk of the front lines and the mining area in the rear there would be glimpses, good enough for Pissarro and Sisley, of fields bright with poppies and lanes beginning to smell of honeysuckle. When we were given a few days' rest, we went back to a mining village that had an enormous slag-heap. Far away, behind the ridge they held, the Germans had a great naval gun that had the range of this village. The shell it fired was of such a monstrous calibre that you could easily hear it coming, like an aerial express. We would be hanging about, smoking and talking, enjoying the sunshine and the quiet, when suddenly we would hear this monster coming. There was only one safe place, behind the slag-heap, and everybody would run for it pell-mell. *Shirrr-brirrr-bump!* There it went, and we would come from behind the slag-heap and see the smoke clearing and another six houses gone. Fortunately that gun did no night-work, and we did not really mind it during the day. Up in the line, what we did mind, what soon began to get us down, were the *Minenwerfers*, the big trench-mortars; and at Souchez we always appeared to have the *Minenwerfer* specialists against us. Often we asked for their attention; not us, the ordinary infantry who had to stay in the front line, but the Brigade, the Division, the Corps, the Army. What happened all too often was that our own specialists would rush their Stokes guns up into the support trenches, blast away for quarter of an hour, and then hurry off with their infernal things to where their transport was waiting. Pampered and heartless fellows – this is how we regarded them – lunatic experts who had to interfere, off they went to some back area, to roofs and beds and *estaminets*, beer and wine, chips and eggs; while we poor devils, left behind in holes in the ground, now had to face the anger of the Boches they had been strafing. The *Minenwerfer* teams got to work on us. Up and then down came those monstrous canisters of high explosive, making hell's own din when they landed, blasting or burying us. If there was any infantryman who was not afraid of these things, who was not made uneasy by any rumours they would shortly be arriving, I never met him. Perhaps because they were such short-range affairs, perhaps because if you were on the alert, looking and listening hard, you could just dodge them, perhaps because they made such a hellish row, they frightened us more than bullets, bombs, shells of all calibres. And in and around Souchez we crouched below a nest of them.

So one day it had to happen. It was June now, hot again, thirsty weather, a lot of chalk dust about, and we were in the front line on a beautiful morning. The platoon rations had just come up. I sent Private O'Neill down the communication trench to bring up some water – and sixteen years went by before we saw each other again. I helped a young soldier, who had only just joined us out there, to take the rations into a dugout, not a deep dugout but a small one hollowed out of the parapet. In this dugout I began sorting out the bread, meat, tea, sugar, tinned milk, and so on, to give each section its proper share, a tricky little job. I had done it many times before, hardly ever to anybody's complete satisfaction; but on this morning I suspect that it saved my life. After the explosion when everything had caved in, nobody was certain I was there, but several fellows knew the platoon rations were in there somewhere: that stuff would have to be dug out. There I was then, deciding on each section's share, when I heard a rushing sound, and I knew what it meant and knew, though everything had gone into slow motion, I had no hope of getting away before the thing arrived. Just as on earlier and later occasions when I have thought all was up, the first shrinking in terror was followed, as I went into the new slow time, by a sense of detachment. I believe from what I learnt long afterwards that the *Minenwerfer* landed slap in the trench, two or three yards away. All I knew at the time was that the world blew up.

4

I do not remember how and by what route I travelled from the front line at Souchez to the military hospital at North Evington, a suburb of Leicester. Any man who was ever around, not as close as I was but, let us say, about three times the distance, when a big German trench-mortar went off, will agree that I was lucky to be carted away in one piece. Had I been as near as that and out in the trench, I would have been blown to bits. As it was, though I had some minor injuries from the dugout caving in, was partly deaf, and ran a high temperature that kept me in bed for some weeks, no parts of me were missing and there was nothing wrong with me that prolonged treatment and rest would not cure. I was lucky in that war and have never ceased to be aware of the fact.

The first clear recollection I have of the North Evington hospital shows me my parents, arriving out of a haze, staring at me mistily across the bed. Day by day for ten months or so, they had probably had a worse time than I had had, wondering what was happening, waiting for those letters that now I realise said too little, never really tried to grasp their hands. *Speak now and I will answer. . . .* But too often we don't speak in this sense, certainly not in my family. We are affectionate and have plenty to say on general topics, but never have we spoken from heart to heart, not I to my father, not my children to me, and so far perhaps not their children to them. With us the Lord our God is an inhibited God, visiting the awkward silences and unspoken endearments of the fathers upon the children unto the third and fourth generation.

There may be people who enjoy a hospital life, but at no time have I been one of them. Once my temperature began to come down and I was no longer wandering in the land of delirium, I longed to be out of that bed, that ward. Opposite my bed was a table on which there was a gramophone, and on the turntable of this gramophone was a record of a baritone singing 'Sussex, Sussex by the Sea!' Everybody who went past halted a moment or two to start the gramophone going, but nobody ever changed the record. Lying there, forbidden to move, indeed in no condition to take action, I had to endure hours of that cursed instrument grinding out 'Sussex, Sussex by the Sea!' Now and again a small piano arrived and with it some well-meaning but not brilliant local talent, mostly wobbly sopranos. One of them, not remarking how we glared from our beds, nearly always sang that drivelling refrain:

We don't want to lose you
But we think you ought to go,
For your King and your Country
Both need you so.

The First War, unlike the Second, produced two distinct crops
of songs : one for patriotic civilians, like that drivel above; the
other, not composed and copyrighted by anybody, genuine
folk song, for the sardonic front-line troops. Of these some
were bawdy, like the famous 'Mademoiselle from Armentières'
and 'The Ballad of Bollocky Bill the Sailor and the Fair Young
Maiden'; some were lugubrious and homesick, without
patriotic sentiment of any kind, like 'I Want to go Home';
others were sharply concerned with military life from the stand-
point of the disillusioned private. The best of these, with its
rousing chorus of 'I know where he is', asked in one lilting verse
after another if you wanted the officer, the sergeant-major, the
quartermaster-sergeant, and so on, and then told you what
these nuisances were up to. The last verse and chorus, however, changed the form and the mood, for here the battalion
was the subject, and after 'I know where it is' was repeated
quietly there came the final reply :

It's hanging on the old barbed wire.
I've seen 'em, I've seen 'em
Hanging on the old barbed wire.

And to this day I cannot listen to it unmoved. There is a flash
of pure genius, entirely English, in that 'old', for it means that
even that devilish enemy, that death-trap, the wire, has somehow been accepted, recognised and acknowledged almost with
affection, by the deep rueful charity of this verse. I have looked
through whole anthologies that said less to me.

From the hospital at North Evington, before the summer
was over, I was sent to convalesce to a country house in Rutland. It was an unbelievable move. After all, the hospital was
like the one I had known at Le Tréport; it was, so to speak,
only a clean white extension of the war world I had lived in for
the past year; it might almost have been an immense hygienic
dugout. The country house in Rutland was in another world,
outside the war, but it was not at all the one I had known before
I enlisted. It belonged to light comedy and those trifling
novels, not without charm and an appealing absurdity, that
were one of the literary fashions before 1914. Even Rutland
itself was as near to being an imaginary county as the map of
England would allow. A country house there did not seem to
be anything that could appear on an Army Order. It was as if
one end of the vast military machine dissolved into fantasy. I
travelled to Rutland, no distance from Leicester of course,
wearing the sky-blue coat and pants, the white shirt and
scarlet tie of the wounded and convalescent in the First War,
sensible enough, nevertheless the gaudiest outfit I have ever
worn in a public conveyance.

I arrived at the country house at a moment of crisis there.
People were rushing in and out of rooms and slamming doors
like characters in a farce; there were exclamations and ex-
postulations caught in passing, and glimpses of beautiful
V.A.D.s melting into tears. One Alfred, let us say, was being
mentioned. 'No, no, Alfred, *please!*' could be heard when doors
were left open too long; undoubtedly the crisis raged round
Alfred. I felt I ought not to be there, though nobody said so.
On the other hand, I also felt that I was outside reality just as I
had been so often in and around the front line, though here of
course I was out at the other end, where there were doves and
roses and lawns like carpets. Before the day was out, one of the
beautiful V.A.D.s told me what had happened. Alfred was the

butler, nothing to do with us convalescents but still there waiting upon the elderly couple who owned the house and lived in the superior quarters of it. He was a young butler, large and rather handsome in a portly butlerish style; and when charged with getting one of the maids in the family way he had admitted the offence, had broken down in his remorse, and had then put an end to any further reproaches by threatening to destroy himself. A full chorus of panic-stricken females, consisting of the family, housekeeper, cook, assorted maids, nurse, the starched and red-crossed debs, had implored him to forgive them their cruel reproaches by abandoning this plan to commit suicide, and, almost as a favour, he had agreed. This was the feminine household view. We convalescents, brutalised by military life and shellfire, did not share it. 'Dodgin' the column, that Alfred,' we told one another. 'An artful sod if I ever saw one, Alfred is.'

There were about ten of us in the house, doing all right except from a strictly regimental and medical point of view, from which we were magically far removed. This was a dream of a cushy billet, and we knew it. The doctor who came round once a day looked and behaved as if he were about eighty, but an unusually amiable eighty: it was said of him that he had treated a village girl for dropsy until her advanced pregnancy forced itself upon his notice. So long as our wounds and ailments did not suddenly take a turn for the worse, this was the doctor for us. The one professional nurse in the house belonged to the same series; nobody could have been in sharper contrast to the regular Army nursing sisters, terrors who preferred your agony to an untidy ward. She was plump, middle-aged, spectacled, beaming, like a drawing of a motherly type in a children's story, and she always took our temperature at night five minutes after we had swallowed our hot cocoa. She was assisted, sketchily, by those V.A.D. girls, who were all

County, with pretty faces straight out of the *Tatler* and *Bystander*, and so spotless and vivid in their uniforms that they looked like nurses in a musical comedy. They were friendly but not flirtatious, regarding most of us as heroic peasants. Early in our acquaintance, one of them advised me solemnly to take up polo. This was naïve enough – and I had to tell her that all I possessed would probably not buy a half-share in a pony, let alone a string of them and all the rest of it – but even she could not have seen me as a peasant when she recommended polo, could she? No, I soon achieved a higher status, not because I claimed to be a writer, perhaps had a flashing eye and could talk about all manner of things, but because I played the piano.

I played badly, as I have already suggested. When a married daughter of the family came to stay, bringing her violin, I was invited into the drawing-room – well out of bounds for us Tommies – and there made a desperate hash out of trying to play at sight the piano part of César Franck's sonata for violin and piano. With a few other pieces, merely supplying an accompaniment, I managed better. There were no love passages between us. She was a thin and nervous woman, probably in her middle thirties, so in my sight almost a neurotic hag; and ten to one I looked to her a sweating oaf. For a recital of Chopin I had neither the technique nor the temperament, nor for that matter the audience; but for an hour or two slam-banging away at songs from musical comedies, music-hall ditties, students' songbook choruses, probably I had no equal then in Rutland. I was dashing, tireless, and what I could not remember I could improvise. This very minor accomplishment, not to be mentioned to cultured persons, served me well all the time I was in the Army: I was the Orpheus of recreation rooms, *estaminets*, convalescent camps, mess anterooms. I remember my friend George Gordon,

Professor of English at Oxford and then Master of Magdalen, telling me how useful the piano had been to him in the war; and he, by his own confession, was not in my class, being a mere vamper by ear, chained to the tedious optimism of C Major. Once in the Second War, late in 1940, I was in Glasgow to do a broadcast. I was drinking whisky with the Lord Provost when a message came through that men rescued from a torpedoed liner were in a hall, waiting for the train that would take them to London. They were getting restless, still hardly out of shock, and it was important that they should not wander away. Would the Lord Provost talk to them, to keep them there? So he went, and I went with him, and when he had no more to say I banged away at the piano and led the choruses; and they were still there, roaring away, when at last we could announce their train was now ready for them. Now in 1916, in that country house in Rutland, I not only played the piano but, instead of distilling Georgian poetry out of the borders that blazed in the garden, the unfamiliar silence and starlight of August and September nights far from the line, I also organised a little concert party. Rutland had tried to entertain us; we would now entertain Rutland.

No doubt we were terrible. But we amused ourselves and a great many other people, during a bad hour, when the slaughter-house of the Somme was working overtime. The only person who did not like us, and indeed hated me, was a dark and savage-looking sergeant – he had been in the police at Penang – who joined us for convalescence about then, felt out of it, wanted to claim authority he did not have, and anyhow was obviously one of The Enemy. He was a type I rarely failed to encounter wherever I went in the Army, nearly always enjoying some sort of authority; the mutual dislike was immediate and never changed except for the worse; it was The Enemy. But though this sergeant blustered and sneered, he could do us no harm, and soon he vanished. I have in front of me now a postcard photograph of our tiny troupe, five of us ready to do our hunting-song number, a favourite in that hunting country and one easy to dress because we were able to borrow authentic hats and pink coats. The faces of the other four are here, and just as clear to me, after more than forty-five years, are their voices, mannerisms, personalities. As end men, wearing top hats, are Beldon, a solemn Durham miner, the oldest of us, who sang ballads in a strangulated high tenor, and Lillystone, a large and good-natured East Ender who could not do anything very much and called himself our stage manager. Between them are Church, wearing cap, pink coat, imitation top boots and a false moustache, who came from the South somewhere and had a cousin who was a well-known mimic on the Halls; Aldrich, a lively and cheeky Cockney, also in hunting rig, perched on a rocking-horse and holding up a toy trumpet; and me, with a bushy false moustache and a toy stuffed dog (no, not hound) under each arm. God knows – and I cannot remember – what we sounded like and when the fun began, if ever it did! But between us we made something, breaking the fixed consumer attitude. And I take this, whatever the politicians and advertising men may say, to be the right way to live.

Sometimes as a troupe, sometimes with our fellow convalescents, we were invited to visit the great mansions scattered about the East Midlands. There we were given a high tea ceremoniously below stairs. The butler would preside at one end of the long table, the housekeeper at the other. The footmen had gone, but there was still no shortage of maids of all ranks. The kitchens and pantries and servants' halls in these mansions were often like magnificent stage sets, with pans and utensils in rows, beginning in giant sizes, with vistas of silver and pewter and burnished copper. Is it too late now to do what

Gilbert and Sullivan ought to have done – to write a comic
opera in which all the action passes below stairs in one of those
enormous country houses? I remember the ceremony of those
high teas and the amount we devoured, for the food at our own
place was good enough but doled out carefully, no heaping of
plates there. What I do not remember, sitting at those long
tables between butler and housekeeper, listening to portentous chit-chat about the family, was feeling any social
resentment, any revolutionary impulses. The truth is, perhaps
because I was still not a fit man, was not completely out of that
bomb-blasted dugout yet, everything that happened to me
around there was both absurd and dreamlike, not in any world
I could take seriously. I had been blown out of the bitter chalk
of Artois into some tale of roses and mown grass and dawns
without gunfire: I could take a butler or two.

In autumn rain I left Rutland and its cast of unlikely
characters, its summer day's dream, to report at the depot in
Halifax, wedged firmly in reality. From there I was dispatched for further treatment to a convalescent camp at Ripon.
There I was miserable, like everybody else I knew. It was a
bad camp, so bad that not long afterwards, I believe, the men
mutinied. There was too much mud, too many unnecessary
restrictions, too many P.T. instructors swelling their chests,
which had never known a front-line parapet, in their red-and-
black-striped jerseys, and bellowing at better men, as we
thought, to look alive and jump to it. We realised that we
ought to attempt some physical training, but we resented
being treated like recruits by these swaggerers who had
never been further than the P.T. School at Aldershot. To hell
with them and their jumping to it! Confined to camp, because
of some recent rumpus, we muttered and growled in corners,
making plans to get out of this hole by hook or crook, though
we had all heard rumours of what happened in the terrible

'glass house', the military prison where they systematically wore down your resistance, broke your spirit.

One of our most notable pieces of self-deception is that we English on all levels, at all times and places, are an easy-going people, kindly disposed whatever the situation, unlike callous and cruel foreigners. This may be true of our ordinary relationships, though even there we have a bad record in our treatment of children; it is certainly not true of official England, which often turns on us a very harsh visage. We still hang men when most other countries have abolished capital punishment. There are demands that we should start flogging again, even restoring the terrible 'cat' (cat o' nine tails, a sadistic inspiration) that in a few strokes tears a man's back to red ribbons. Until recently many of our prisons were far more inhumane than most prisons abroad. And in the earlier part of the First War, when the Services were crowded with eager volunteers, decent young men who had not been brought out of gaols or collared by the press gang, those Services retained brutal forms of punishment discontinued by those inferior and cruel foreigners. One of them I remember was Field Punishment Number One, in which a man was tied to a gun-carriage, out in the open and unable to move for hour after hour. It was dropped later in the war, together with some other savage anachronisms, but not before much damage had been done to English bodies and spirit. We have in English society a large number of men on a certain level, not at the top but a long way from the bottom, usually in authority somewhere, who have been insensitive and brutalised from boyhood, who are psychological misfits and haters of life. Drop out of a clean-collar-and-bank-balance style of living, even if only by enlisting as we did, and these types come looming up. Take the wobbling lid off, give them a free hand, and even now they would show us a nasty thing or two.

[118]

After a few sullen weeks, perhaps in less time than that, a trainload of us was removed from Ripon to a larger and better convalescent camp just outside Alnwick in Northumberland. I forget how many months I was up there; it seems like years, an exile in some cosier Siberia. I needed no more treatment of any sort but was not yet passed fit, and anyhow I had now applied for a commission. The little old town was pleasant enough, and I knew some equally pleasant people there. At first I stared in romantic awe at Alnwick Castle, more like my idea of one than any other I had yet seen. I stared no longer when I learnt that most of what I saw had never known Hotspur and the Middle Ages, had in fact been built in the eighteenth century by a man called Smith who married into the Percy family. If the camp itself had any particular character, I have forgotten what it was. Being large and heterogeneous, it was a good camp for dodging such parades and fatigues as there might be. Every morning for weeks, I attended the full parade with a group of fellow dodgers, and at the sergeant-major's cry of 'Fatigue parties, dismiss!' I marched off my little party, back to the hut to do nothing. A corporal of the West Yorks, needing some leave and having been refused it, bluffed his way home by sheer magnificent impudence. He collected about a dozen West Riding men who also wanted a spell at home, though they had not a single leave pass and railway warrant between them, and marched them smartly to the station and barked at them to board the train. At Newcastle and York they had to change trains to reach the West Riding, and both these stations swarmed with 'redcaps' (the military police) ready to pounce upon any soldier on his own and looking a bit shifty, demanding to see his leave pass and railway warrant. But each time this corporal marched his party on to the right platform, stood them at ease while waiting for the train, and looked so regimental and important that he was never challenged, so took them all home. They may have had a few bits of paper to show if necessary. In the back room of a pub in Alnwick, two or three artful characters, soldiers not civilians, did a fine trade in forged leave passes and railway warrants. I knew a corporal who, having been once given a warrant for some obscure place in Cornwall or Cumberland, never gave it up, and used it for going by train anywhere he pleased, nobody knowing or caring if he was on the way to this mysterious place or not. I was sent, with two men, to bring a man, absent without leave, from Wakefield, and we took the best part of a week over the job. They were having a party at his house when we arrived there. 'Nay, yer won't want him for a day or two, will yer?' they cried. 'What about comin' on Thursday?'

We were now well into 1917, the only full year of the war I was never near the front, never out of England. It was a sort of dead time for me. I was neither dodging the war nor anxious any longer to be a good soldier in it. I did a little writing, but my heart was not in it, because my heart was not in anything. Some local dame, well-to-do, earnest, cultured, whose name I have forgotten, offered a money prize for the best piece by one of these poor fellows at Alnwick Camp; so I bestirred myself and got the money, which I probably needed for beer. I drank a lot of beer then. Many nights, either in the canteen or a town pub, I spent with a sardonic and argumentative character who had lost an arm; he was a newspaperman from Leeds called Lance Grocock; and he and I talked and talked and sank pint after pint until we felt stupefied. Nobody should drink beer for hours; it drowns a man's wits and finally blurs any sharp outline of character. I think mine, young as I was, began to feel blurred a little. Everybody with any intelligence must remember a time when personality touched rock bottom, hoping for nothing, desiring nothing, just getting by. Those months in 1917, first at Alnwick and then at Tynemouth, were to me such a time. I existed without meaning, depth and insight. My sensations were blunted; my intuitions were valueless; my feelings came without colour and music; my thought lost any edge and penetration it may ever have had. Compared with the youth I had been two years before, I was riff-raff. I might have been one of our anti-heroes born before his time.

During the weeks, I forget how many, when I had left Alnwick, having been passed fit at last, and was temporarily attached to the Third Battalion on Tyneside, waiting to be sent as a cadet to an O.T.C., I seemed to be in an ugly army, on the edge of a rotten war. The Enemy was there, with hate at first sight, with attempts almost every day to trap me into making some mistake that would finish me for a commission. If I made a single friend, then I have forgotten him, and this is not likely. Drafts of officers, noncoms and men were being sent to the Front. I do not know what happened with the officers; I was out of touch with the men, all strangers; but I saw what went on among the noncoms, especially those who were rather older than I was, many of them married, more or less settled in the town. To be threatened with being put on the next draft, to some of these men, was like being rung up by Murder Inc. Their only chance of escape was to persuade, let us say, The Enemy, to leave their names off the list. Sometimes it took money; sometimes a pretty young wife had to be obliging. I loathed what I saw and heard inside the regiment; and if there was anything happening just then outside it, anywhere in the neighbourhood, to uplift the heart of man, then I missed it. Even so, I was lucky. I might have been at Passchendaele, where Haig, who ought to have gone up there himself or gone home, was slicing my whole generation into sausage meat held above a swill bucket. Once in New York in the Thirties I saw a musical sourly entitled *Hurray for What?* We ought to have thought of it earlier and used it for Victory Parades.

The 16th Officer Cadet Battalion – I think that was its name – to which I was posted, much to my relief, was at Kinmel Park Camp in North Wales. We were worked hard there, but I enjoyed it all. I was jerked out of my apathy, my slack habits of mind and body. I made no close friends among my fellow cadets – there was hardly time – but they were pleasant to work and live with. The Enemy did not show up among the officers and instructors. I played football again, for my company team. I wrote some satirical odds and ends, both for print and performance. A great deal of what we were taught I could not take seriously, not simply because I was not really a military type, though of course I was not, but also because I believed much of it to be out of date, merely an attempt to improve on what we did in the Boer War. All that musketry, for example, in which one of our chief instructors was a major in Orders, perhaps a parson-schoolmaster before the war, a cheerful pagan who was fond of referring to 'we old Bisley bull-punchers', hardly an ecclesiastical Order. It seemed to me that the rifle was all very well in frontier skirmishes, but the war we were in was chiefly an affair of machine-guns, bombs, mortars, shellfire. And I had a sharp dislike, together with much mistrust, of all that he-man guff about 'the spirit of the bayonet'. We might have saved about half a million lives if we had forgotten all those campaigns against Fuzzy-wuzzies and Boer commandos and had given some thought to the German General Staff. Not that our platoon commander, though an oldish regular, was so limited in his outlook. His name was Tredennick, and he was an odd fish, conscientious but probably a bit cracked, and when he got going on strategy, his eyes glittering and the words pouring out, whole continents, not yet fully involved, rose and took to arms, Asia rushed to meet Africa, and soon, while we lit our pipes and stayed out of the rain, the globe was on fire. We were back at school, dangling the bait we knew the master could not resist, triumphantly wasting time.

We dined in turn at the officers' mess, to prove we did not always eat peas with a knife. We sat for an examination. All but an unfortunate few were passed out and duly commissioned. Out of the allowance we were given we bought greatcoats and British warms, tunics and Sam Browne belts. We were officers free for ever from cookhouse fatigues and carrying coils of barbed wire. I was commissioned to the Devon Regiment, and after a few days' swagger at home I arrived at its headquarters and barracks at Devonport, as new and shy and glossy as a bridegroom.

5

Except for a few courses at camps in Cornwall, I was there at the barracks in Devonport for months and months, until almost the end of that summer of 1918. Although it seemed to me, after what I had known so far, the life of Reilly, I made no attempt to avoid being drafted out to the Front. I was ready to go if I was wanted. Perhaps because all but one of the Devon battalions were not in France then, were serving without any great loss of men in distant theatres of war, I was not wanted. After tents, barns, trenches and wooden huts, and the greasy stew and congealing bacon that went with them, those barracks were four-star quarters. We lived well, dined with the regimental silver and with the regimental band playing outside. I got to know that band very well. We junior officers were supposed to turn out and be drilled, in a highly elaborate and quite useless fashion as if we might have to join one of Marlborough's armies, by a mad old Marine sergeant, who had drilled himself out of his mind. The adjutant, discovering that I was dodging these insane parades, came roaring up – in one of those scarlet-faced professional fits of bad temper that must have ruined the blood pressure of many regular officers – and told me that from now on I would be in charge of funeral parties. Why he thought this some form of punishment I cannot imagine. There was a large military hospital in Plymouth and hardly a day passed without a death there; and the bodies were sometimes buried in the local cemetery, but more often than not they had to be taken to the station and ceremonially entrained. It was our duty to supply a firing party for the cemetery or a guard to present arms at the station; with it went the regimental band, a sergeant who knew all the drill and gave the commands, and an officer who really did nothing. I was that officer. Morning after morning we slow-marched to the station, where often there were weeping relatives on the platform; we gave the coffin a last salute; then off we went, marching briskly, the band playing a lively tune. After taking part in this ironical piece, I considered myself free – without reporting back to the adjutant – for the remainder of the day. If it were a fine afternoon I might stroll along the Hoe and wonder if the bright-eyed girls were married to naval officers. After dinner I rarely stayed boozing in the mess; usually I went into Devonport or Plymouth, perhaps to a cinema, rich then in new Chaplin and custard-pie short films, or to a music-hall, where variety was then in its Indian summer, brilliant and dying.

It was three years after I had first gone to France that a little batch of us subalterns were given our orders and crossed to Boulogne. We sailed by day in a fantastic American ship that might have been fetched from the Mississippi. We were the only British aboard among thousands of American troops, new, raw and hearty, with nothing in their mode of address to distinguish their rank. A vast bunch of Kiwanis or Shriners might have been off on a river picnic. Way up on the top deck – it was a tall narrow, sort of ship with a lot of decks – a big band, with more than its share of those gleaming sousaphones, blared and clashed out ragtime. It seemed a hell of a way to sail to a war but not completely ridiculous, not without a suggestion of something more generous and heart-warming, much closer to the democracy we boasted about on our side, than anything we had known before. On that daft but not altogether inglorious troopship, I realised afterwards, I was for the first time in America.

Where all those 'doughboys' went I do not know, but our little group had to join what was left of a battalion of dismounted yeomanry. It was somewhere beyond Peronne, and took some finding in the dust and heat, on roads jammed with transport. There were about six of us, I think, mostly going out for the first time; and I never knew what happened to three of them, but the two I knew best, friends I made at Devonport, were killed within a few days. Again I was lucky, or perhaps by this time unconsciously artful. The battalion, which I never really took in as a unit, was far below strength but still up in front, attacking. We were in a narrow railway cutting one evening – at least the only troops I knew anything about were there – and into it the Germans dropped a lot of gas shells. Gas-masked myself, I ran about to make sure the men were wearing their masks, a thing they hated to do. No doubt some gas seeped through my mask, as the doctors said afterwards; but I must add here that later that night, when we crept out of the cutting, ready to move forward just after dawn, I drank a good many tots of rum, which now, unlike 1915 and 1916, was in generous supply.

We went to the attack in the early morning, on a front much too wide for us, and there was one of those very thick mists,

dense as fog, common in September. After ten minutes – and
you may put it down to gas, rum or carelessness, just as you
please – I had lost the whole battle, which I could hear all
round me but could not see. I was wandering about, befogged
inside and out, entirely alone. But I must have been more or
less advancing, not retreating, for a figure came looming up
through the whiteness, and I saw it was a German and waved
my revolver at him. After all, he was not to know that I had
been on two revolver courses and never could hit anything. He
was a lad about sixteen, who ought to have been several
hundred miles away, putting his school books into a satchel.
He raised his arms, poor lad, and made gibbering noises. I
tried to look a little less idiotic than I felt, and pointed sternly
in what I hoped was the direction of the British and not the
German Army, and off he trotted, leaving me alone once more
in the mist, wondering where to find the battle. I never did
catch up with it. My head going round, too short of breath to
move any further, I took a rest in a shellhole, where I was
found by a couple of stretcher-bearers. So much for my last
glimpse of action in the Great War.

From the base hospital, where I had listened for days and
days and days to the autobiography of a brown little doctor
from Arizona, I went to the Medical Board Base Depot in
Rouen. (I have described this autumn of 1918 before, in the
opening non-fiction passages of a story I wrote, thirty-three
years ago, *The Town Major of Miraucourt*.) You waited there
until the medical board decided to see you, and often after that
until it decided to see you again. Meanwhile, we officers
earned our keep there by censoring vast piles of letters or
going to distant huts and paying out troops who always seemed
to come from the Hebrides or the West Indies: hour after
hour some purple-faced quartermaster-sergeant yelled outlandish names. The depot officers' mess was like a railway

refreshment room towards the end of an hysterical Bank Holiday; even at breakfast-time it looked as if an excursion trainload had just left it; but it had a wonderful supply of those small export bottles of Guinness at one franc the bottle. We ordered more and more of these bottles and became involved in long and idiotic arguments, all with men one had never seen before and never wanted to see again.

The medical board decided I was B2, unfit for active service but fit for something. I was told to report at the other side of the town. There I found a very neat little colonel; the depressing house in which I found him, and its Rouen back-street, came straight out of French fiction of the Eighties. The colonel was fighting it all – tooth-and-nailbrush; he was a responsible and solemn English gentleman in one of the waste places; he spoke to me gravely about dinner and dress. The Labour Corps Depot, to which I had been sent for duty, was itself a large factory building, swarming with men who never seemed quite real, ghostly perhaps because they were so tired, so bored. Only the sergeants, spick and span, terrific saluters and callers to attention, were familiar figures; they could be found at all depots and bases, keeping the old flag flying, the brass buttons polished; real professional soldiers, waiting for this monstrous amateur affair, this bloodthirsty melodrama of bomber bank clerks and machine-gunner gardeners, to blow itself to pieces. This factory had been turned into a lunatic labour exchange. There we had only to receive, in correct triplicate, an indent for any form of labour, and we would supply it. Entertainers were our favourite commodity; I soon wangled my way into this branch of the business. If the Fourth Army wanted two comedians, three conjurers, a couple of female impersonators, it sent us a wire saying so; then we paraded the most likely specimens, tried one or two out on the stage (we had an excellent stage on the third floor), and packed them off by the next train. Fresh relays of comedians, baritones, female impersonators, arrived every day or so, had their kits and paybooks inspected, and were handed over to the beery and brilliantined sergeants. I began to feel like a variety agent in uniform, or a man dreaming he was one.

During dinner, with the little colonel at the head of the table, correct but at ease, we talked a good deal about the war, which was beginning to wobble. A report came of an armistice, and the little colonel bought us all champagne on the strength of it, and was furious when the report was denied. The streets smelled of autumn, and dead leaves drifted down the canal. We existed now on that melancholy underside of French life. One day, taking the afternoon off, I went walking along a wide straight track through a wood; there came towards me, like a figure in an old-fashioned painting, sad and with too much brown in it, a hobbling crone, who when we met and I gave her good-day, stopped, grinned toothlessly, and produced a small document for me to read: it was a licence entitling her to ply her trade as a prostitute in Rouen and district. I told her, in the fluent bad French I spoke then and can no longer command, that I was not in the mood. A character from English not French fiction arrived to share my room, a tall, thin subaltern with a slight squint who came from Birmingham; he could talk of nothing but the musical-comedy actress he had once met there, no other than the Nellie Taylor I had watched with joy and pain four years before. A smokiness came in the morning and returned in the late afternoon; our suburb was besieged by dank air; the men were more ghostly than ever as they limped up and down the stairs of the mad factory. I inspected kits, sent for conjurers, talked about the war or Nellie Taylor; and then the genuine Armistice took us by surprise after so many false reports, and we had to hurry to get drunk enough to go shouting and reeling round the town. I can remember trying to work myself up into the right Bacchanalian mood, trying to ignore the creeping shadows, the mysterious rising tide of regret and sadness, which I think all but the simplest men suffer from on these occasions.

Two or three mornings later, I was told to report for duty at a prisoner-of-war camp near Calais, and to take a party of men with me. This was the journey, Rouen to Calais, that took us about three days, mostly spent in a motionless and window-less train in some siding, where we used the locomotive's boiler for a constant service of tea. During my first evening in the P.O.W. camp mess, I decided I had run out of luck, for here was a collection of fellows I disliked on sight. Later, when I had retired to my thin-walled cubicle, I overheard, not being able to help it, two of them discussing me in the next cubicle, making it clear they did not like the look and sound of me either. This did not upset me because I had never considered myself a charmer, and most of these types, who had dug them-selves in here long ago, looked to me like artful base wallahs. The company to which I was attached was commanded by a red-faced major, not himself a regular soldier – he had done some easy job 'out East' – but closely related to the red-tabbed Top. From the first he obviously considered me an opinionated young North Country cad, and I thought him a pompous ass who did not even try to do properly the soft job he had been given. And on these terms, living in close quarters, we were to be associated for the next three-and-a-half months, though fortunately he gave himself a lot of leave.

This big camp supplied prison labour, working in shifts round the clock, for the largest quarries I had ever seen, greyish-white canyons, from which had come the road-metal used by the Chinese coolies. I rather enjoyed my turn at the late-night shift in these quarries, where I had little to do but marvel at the eerie effects of the brilliant artificial lighting down there, the dazzling cliffs and battlements, the dead-black shadows, the glimpses of distant groups who looked like ants at work. The German prisoners were not driven hard; their living conditions were not bad; they were fed better than they would have been in their own army, far better than their folks at home, whose parcels, which we had to open and inspect, were pathetic offerings of *ersatz* sausage and all manner of crumbling muck. Yet just because they *were* prisoners, because the psychological effect of their status was so strong, most of them had the drawn and large-eyed look of men overworked, beaten and half-starved. In point of fact they were far more frightened of their own sergeant-major characters – iron men with Iron Crosses, Kaiser moustaches, terrible rasping words of command – than they were of us, the unmilitary amateur British. Though these iron characters showed me tremendous respect, as if I were a general, I went a little in awe of them myself. Later, when our company was on its own, far from these quarries, and it was Christmas, I remember how astonished I was, paying an official visit to the German warrant officers' tiny mess, to discover these four military monsters sitting round a very small illuminated Christmas tree, deep in a sentimental reverie before they caught sight of me and jumped quivering to attention, banging their heels. There was all Germany in that little scene.

Long before Christmas, however, our company received orders to move up to the Lille-Roubaix-Tourcoing area, to do salvage work. By chance, the major and the lieutenant senior to me being away, I was in charge of the company when these orders arrived, and I had to be responsible for the move. We had between six and seven hundred prisoners, and about eighty British troops, all men no longer fit for active service. Though the fighting was over, conditions were no easier, perhaps rather more chaotic, so that problems of transport,

rationing, supplies, medical services, were no joke, especially
with such an odd mixture involving seven to eight hundred
men. This was easily the most responsible job that had come
my way in the Army, and it lasted for a couple of weeks or so
and I enjoyed every moment of it, planning and working hard
with several decent and conscientious senior noncoms. I
cannot believe there was in me somewhere a master of
logistics, a first-class staff officer; I make no claim to any
peculiar merit; but I must set on record the fact that I did the
job and for once, in my four-and-a-half years of army knock-
about, really enjoyed doing it. We had to march the company
through Tourcoing, which had had years of German occupation, and its citizens lined the streets to curse and scream at
our columns of prisoners, whom we had to guard not against
possible escape but lynching. We ended up in the country
outside, packed into a few big barns. It was then, after a few
days, I ran into trouble, finally picking a quarrel, a most
enjoyable shemozzle, with the Fifth Army: *A Four-round
Contest between Subaltern One, in the blue corner, and Army
H.Q. in the red-and-gilt corner.*

After more than forty years it is easy to over-simplify or to
exaggerate, but this brief report of the contest is as true as I
can make it. Round one: still temporarily in charge of the
company, I receive an Army order telling me to move it to a
given map reference, the chosen site for a camp under canvas.
And it is now early December. I go to this place, find it pitted
with shellholes and waterlogged, and point out there must
have been some mistake, a wrong map reference. Round two:
Army informs me in writing that no mistake has been made,
that I have had my orders and any further delay will not be
tolerated. Counter-punching, I reply in writing that the chosen
site is utterly unsuitable even for seven hundred and fifty fit
men, that many of our men, British and Germans, are not fit

and that I have on my hands a number of sick prisoners, some of them running temperatures. Round three: a carload of red tabs and brass hats arrives, important chaps with staring eyes and those voices that are the equivalent in sound of hard stares, and ask what the devil I think I am doing, who the devil I think I am, and that they are giving me one last chance before I find myself facing a court-martial. Covering up and hanging on, in boxing terms, I mutter that the place they have chosen, which I cannot believe they can have seen for themselves, is impossible, that I cannot accept the responsibility of moving these men there, that my war is over and if the Fifth Army wants to court-martial me, let them get on with it. They stare at me again, climb haughtily into the car, and drive off. Fourth and last round: I lead with some smart left jabs, for now I have found, not too far from the site they chose, the wide-spread ruin of a German hut encampment, and promise that if the Army will leave us alone, then, without incurring any expense or demanding any help from the Engineers, out of this wreck my Germans will build their own camp. To my surprise, I am given a grudging consent, along with a few more warnings. Subaltern wins on points.

Not trusting my halting German on this occasion, I addressed the warrant officers and senior noncoms through the chief interpreter, a red-haired schoolmaster from Bavaria, and explained that their men had a chance to build a decent snug camp for themselves, to house them through the winter, if they worked hard and at full speed. Now among these hundreds of prisoners we had scores of skilled men, and, whatever faults the average German may have, he cannot be accused of a lack of application and diligence; and as I bustled around, entirely out of character for once, I saw with delight a new camp, solid and weatherproof, rise almost magically out of those ruins I had discovered. From the morning I planned the move from

Calais until the day this camp was finished, I had lived, most happily too, the sort of life known to men very different in temperament and outlook from me. I had unexpectedly enjoyed glimpses of roads I had never even thought of taking. I had let loose a part of myself I did not even know was there; for a few astonishing and rewarding days I played the man of action not long before settling down, from that time to this, to live by putting words together and passing round the hat.

During the first three months of 1919 I was still with this P.O.W. company, no longer shouldering any real responsibility, glowering at the major, who now kept popping into Lille to visit a 'pretty little French gal', drinking a bit too much out of boredom, and now feeling more like a trapped civilian than any kind of soldier. We officers round there were now sharply divided into those, like me, who ached to leave the Army and get on with their real lives, and senior men, like the major, who knew when they were on to a good thing and dreaded the bowler hat. (There was a rumour, before I left, that it was taking three full colonels to run a laundry in Lille.) As he regarded me as a nuisance, the major was glad to forward various applications I made for demobilisation. Finally, I was told I could go home, not because I was already enquiring about an educational grant, but because I had been a casualty three times and came into some category that had a slight priority of release. The day arrived. Our own noncoms, with whom I had worked during that move and camp-building afterwards, seemed genuinely sorry to see me go. 'The only bloody officer we ever had who was any good,' I overheard one of the men say, 'an' now of course he's off.' The Germans, through the red-haired interpreter, made me a solemn speech of thanks and farewell, and presented me with two group photographs, which I still have. No regrets from the Fifth Army or, for that matter, from the major, who now had two subalterns, almost half-witted, prepared to listen to his Eastern 'yarns' and 'pretty little gal' reminiscences ('It's all the etceteras I like best on these occasions, my boy') until their eyes glazed over with whisky and sleep.

There had been trouble on the special night-trains running from Lille to Boulogne, crammed with men from all manner of units on their way to be demobilised. It was said there had been mutinous outbreaks, riot and damage. A lot of these men had had as much of the British Army, with its insistence, often at the wrong time, upon 'keeping the men up to the mark', as they could take. When I reported to the R.T.O. at the station, with the train there already packed and uproarious, I was astonished and shaken to learn from him that not only was no senior officer travelling that night – whether by accident or design I never knew – but that I was in fact the only officer going on that train. I was to be responsible for all the men on it, hundreds and hundreds of them, embittered and sober, roaring and drunk, and responsible too for their seemly arrival at the Boulogne rest camp next morning. It was like suddenly being put in charge of eight circuses, short of pay, food and water. As time passed and we did not pull out, for all these worn-out trains hated to make a move, the atmosphere became curiously sinister. Discipline, always harder to maintain when men were away from their units and came from every branch of the service, had worn so thin you could hear it cracking. It was almost like an army disintegrating in a revolution. I spoke to a few N.C.O.s who seemed steady types, and put it to them that I did not expect anything fancy but that the less trouble we had the sooner we might go home.

Somehow we got by, the train rumbling through the night, in my imagination, like a volcano that might blow up. About the middle of the morning, wonderfully bright and fresh after that train, my mob came tumbling out at Boulogne, break-

fastless and bleary-eyed and not standing any more bloody
nonsense from anybody. They had to be marched to that camp
on the hill. There was not a hope of getting them into two
dressed lines, smartly forming fours (as we did then), and
moving off like a well-drilled infantry column. I gave it out
that the shortest cut home was by way of that camp, that if they
formed themselves into some sort of column of march, followed
me and kept together, no time and temper would be wasted.
So off we went, at any easy pace, for some of the men were
weighed down with kit and in no shape to march properly, and
finally arrived, moving together, at the entrance to the camp.
A little fusspot of an adjutant came charging out, gave me a
glare in passing, and, his voice rising almost to a scream,
began shouting 'Left, right! Left, right!' The men stopped,
looked him over, then either hooted with laughter or told him
what he could do with his *Left, right*. Having created a
situation he did not know how to control, he hurriedly
retired somewhere, not the place where I reported the arrival
of self and party. Had he met the train in this badly-timed
regimental mood, either he or about half the men would not
have seen the camp that day.

This anecdote, a trickle of small beer, is not related here to
suggest that in me a man of action was lost to our time. I was a
bewildered and secretly terrified subaltern of twenty-four,
probably rather naïve even for his years and status, who was
handed a packet one of his seniors should have had, and just got
by after using a little common sense, behaving more like a
civilian than a British officer and temporary gentleman. No,
the spotlight here is on that little adjutant who did not understand what was happening, barked at the wrong time and fled
from his humiliation. He is the last military figure we shall
meet, and he has remained in my mind a symbolic figure. He
will do as well as another to represent what seemed to me to be

wrong from first to last in the British Army of the First War. The development of the familiar 'lions led by donkeys' theme can be left to those indignant younger men now appearing as military historians. But as one who served in that Army, not brilliantly and with a lot of luck but bearing some share of the jeopardy and misery, I should like to add a few observations to the record. So far as that war was won at all – and a negotiated peace in 1916 might have saved our world from one catastrophe after another – I believe that in the end it was chiefly won on the ground by a huge crowd of young Britons who never wanted to be soldiers, hooted at all traditions of military glory, but went on and on, when American forces were still not fully deployed and the French were fading out, with courage and endurance and tenacity we should remember with pride. And nobody, nothing, will shift me from the belief, which I shall take to the grave, that the generation to which I belong, destroyed between 1914 and 1918, was a great generation, marvellous in its promise. This is not self-praise, because those of us who are left know that we are the runts.

The British Army never saw itself as a citizens' army. It behaved as if a small gentlemanly officer class still had to make soldiers out of under-gardeners' runaway sons and slum lads known to the police. These fellows had to be kept up to scratch. Let 'em get slack, they'd soon be a rabble again. So where the Germans and French would hold a bad front line with the minimum of men, allowing the majority to get some rest, the British command would pack men into rotten trenches, start something to keep up their morale, pile up casualties and drive the survivors to despair. This was done not to win a battle, not even to gain a few yards of ground, but simply because it was supposed to be the thing to do. All the armies in that idiot war shovelled divisions into attacks, often as bone-headed as ours were, just as if healthy young men had begun to seem hateful in the sight of Europe, but the British command specialised in throwing men away for nothing. The tradition of an officer class, defying both imagination and common sense, killed most of my friends as surely as if those cavalry generals had come out of the châteaux with polo mallets and beaten their brains out. Call this class prejudice if you like, so long as you remember, as I hope I made plain in an earlier chapter, that I went into that war without any such prejudice, free of any class feeling. No doubt I came out of it with a chip on my shoulder; a big, heavy chip, probably some friend's thigh-bone.

Compelled throughout all my early twenties to live close to all kinds of men, as few of us have to do in civilian life, I came to some rough and ready conclusions that have stayed with me ever since. Out of any ten men chosen at random for you to live with, I decided that, unless the luck was running hard against you, one of them would be your sort, according to your type and temperament, a man you could call a friend, often, sometimes surprisingly, pure gold. The next eight would be average decent fellows, conventional, timid and a bit shuffling perhaps, but capable of responding to a reasonable appeal. The tenth would be no good, except to a saint or a teacher-leader of genius; he would be twisted somewhere inside, malevolent, life-denying, incapable of innocent happiness and so always anxious to smear it, blacken it, destroy it. In an army, and no doubt in many large-scale organisations, this type wants some kind of authority, power over other men, so badly that all too often he gets it, not on any grand scale but sufficient for unwearying malignancy, becoming The Enemy. In an army, or any other service that offers him the cover and opportunity of discipline, he cannot be mistaken. But he exists outside, where names are not taken so quickly and punishment does not follow so fast. He is still around, still busy. But if democracy is not done for, the other eight are still with us. And I am not too old to believe that the first man out of the ten, the one who will understand at once what you are talking about, the possible friend, has vanished. Note that when I refer to men I really mean my own sex. Woman is another, wilder, more entrancing story, not to be told in over-simplified statistics.

This great book of men, which the war opened for me, I read as best I could. Other books – and a lot came my way – I devoured as if they were hot buttered tea-cakes. There were of course times when, however much you might want to read, you had been driven so hard that any kind of shelter and a little warmth closed your eyes and your mind. Except at such times, it was my experience that a bookish soldier, determined and a bit cunning, could spend more time reading than most young civilians. The life did not encourage writing, but you could feast on what other men had written. I think now that I wrote too little and read too much. I came out of the Army a divided young man, one half of him too bookish, the other half, across a gap not properly bridged for years, outside any tradition, committed to nothing except fairly sharp and often comic observation, reading only in that book of men. I came out of the war divided too in another way, not having one attitude towards it, as many men who wrote about it had, but two opposing attitudes I did not know how to reconcile during the years when I too ought to have been writing about it.

Now I believe I can explain what puzzled some people, who began to imagine there was something mysterious, even sinister, about the way in which I, a fertile and energetic writer at least and one who had soldiered as long as most of my fellow writers, shrugged away the war as a grand theme. I could muster some not unreasonable excuses. During my first few years out of the Army, I wanted to get on with my life, to look forward and not back. And I was then giving my bookish half a freer run. Then came, during the next few years, a barrage of war reminiscences and novels – the best of them, by Graves, Sassoon, Blunden, Williamson, Aldington, to name no more, truly and powerfully written by my contemporaries – and I could claim that now I felt I had waited too long. But the real explanation, I believe, is concerned with that other division I have mentioned, those opposed attitudes that I, now merely attempting fiction and no great master of it, did not know how to reconcile. Unlike most of my contemporaries who wrote so well about the war, I was deeply divided between the tragedy and comedy of it. I was as much aware as they were, and as other people born later can never be, of its tragic aspect. I felt, as indeed I still feel today and must go on feeling until I die, the open wound, never to be healed, of my generation's fate, the best sorted out and then slaughtered, not by hard necessity but mainly by huge murderous public folly. On the other hand, military life itself, the whole Army 'carry-on', as we used to say, observed closely, seemed to me essentially comic, the most expensive farce ever contrived. To a man of my temperament it was almost slapstick, so much gigantically solemn, dressed-up, bemedalled custard-pie work, but with tragedy, death, the deep unhealing wound, there in the middle of it. Now then, all you fine fellows who never go down and mine the stuff but sit above, making smart comments on what comes out of the hole, imagine yourselves writing a big novel – it would have to be big – if you were divided at the outset in the way I have described! I agree that if I had ignored this division and hurled myself not *at* but *into* the job – trusting some creative reconciling function of the unconscious, where burning boats perhaps smell sweetly – I might, I just might, have pulled it off. But on my terms, making full allowance for the comic as well as the tragic aspects, nobody else did, and the closest anybody came was not in books written in English or concerned with the British Army. And now it is altogether too late, that is of course for me; any one of our novelists who is fascinated by the First War, believes he has the weight and staying-power to tackle it, and is still only in his middle thirties (a good age for such work), can remind himself that he is as well placed as Tolstoy was when he began *War and Peace*, and indeed has far more material at his disposal. As for me, I let this chance go by, and now I think I was wrong. This does not mean, however, that I wrote other things without being aware of any commitment.

One morning in the early spring of 1919 in some town, strangely chosen, in the Midlands – and I have forgotten both the date and the place – I came blinking out at last into civilian daylight. I made no great resolutions; I was wondering if I could go on a walking tour in the Dales and sell some pieces about it to the *Yorkshire Observer*; I was also deciding to buy a gramophone and some recordings of string quartets. No awards for gallantry had come – or were to come – my way; but I was entitled to certain medals and ribbons. I never applied for them; I was never sent them; I have never had them. Feeling that the giant locusts that had eaten my four-and-a-half years could have them, glad to remember that never again would anybody tell me to carry on, I shrugged the shoulders of a civvy coat that was a bad fit, and carried on.

PART THREE

I Had the Time
(1920 - 1960)

There are two reasons why I have chosen to call this Part Three *I Had the Time*. First: during the past thirty years or so, hundreds of people have told me they could write a good novel, play, book of essays, if only they had the time. Well, I had the time.

The second reason goes deeper. Although we often feel we are outside our time, looking on and wondering, it is all we seem to possess with any certainty. Whether we believe we are immortal spirits, here in exile for a season, or see ourselves as talking mammals, cleverer than any box of monkeys, almost ready to take confusion and despair to another planet, our time is all we have on earth. For each one of us, in just so many hours, sunlight and opportunity vanish for ever. Fed with the necessary data, a computer could work it out in a flash. (Our great-grandchildren will probably be working for the computers: already some of our technologists are on their side, not on ours.) Though there may be something left over, never realised, never fulfilled, never on sea or land, we are what we have done with our time. We are, you might say, stuck with it.

So small, so vulnerable, as he confronts the vast blank universe (whether still expanding or in steady state), Man has his hopes and visions. But better than these, more gallantly defiant, is his sense of irony. If there are no gods to enjoy it with us, then so much the worse for the rest of the cosmos. Here at least, out of the amino-acids, has been distilled the spirit of irony. And I suggest that an English writer in his middle sixties cannot be blamed for relishing this particular spirit – the whisky of the mind. I say English, not even Scots, Welsh, Irish, because in England a writer is regarded with suspicion. He is thought to be either a shirker, left at home with the women when the work has to be done, or a shady type, three parts charlatan to one part black magician. I put him in his middle sixties because that is where I am, not young and bright with promise, not eighty and a Grand Old Man, but an elderly nuisance who has been around too long. So I think the ironic spirit is called for – just one for the road.

Not long ago I published a large book that half-killed me, *Literature and Western Man*. It had a good press: I am not grumbling. But nearly forty years ago, while I was still up at Cambridge, I brought out, through the local booksellers Bowes and Bowes, a little book of undergraduate odds and ends called *Brief Diversions*. It had, in length if not strength, an even better press. The leading reviewers, headed by Edmund Gosse, devoted their columns to it. It had the kind of press that young publishers dream about. One quick tiny shot – and *bang* – the bull's eye! Like a man playing a fruit machine, I cupped my hands for the clanging spill of the jackpot. And nothing happened. No fame, not a hint of it. No sudden big sales, no hasty reprintings. (It took years to sell the small first edition.) But didn't publishers and editors write to this new young man whom Gosse and the rest had reviewed? They did not. Nobody wrote a word. Nothing happened. My career began with an enormous anti-climax.

Perhaps this explains why ever since then I have been suspicious, never smilingly acknowledging good fortune, often appearing surly and ungracious when there was talk of 'your wonderful success'. This is the great Theatre word, found in every first-night telegram, and I have always detested it. Journalists used to ask about success as if it were entirely tangible and concrete, a lump of milk chocolate as big as a lorry. Now a writer may think of himself succeeding or failing with a particular book or play, but never, unless he is a lost soul, does he think of his life and work in terms of success.

There I was in Cambridge then, my little book behind me. My ex-Army grant had never been enough to keep me. I had always had to supplement it with what money I could earn by writing, coaching, and any lecture that would pay a guinea or two. At the end of my second year, when I took my degree, I had a wife to keep – after all, I was now twenty-seven, so many years having vanished in the Army.

My grant still running on, I stayed up for a third year, engaged in post-graduate research on how to make ends meet. But what next? I had the chance of several foreign professorships; they were all in places so small or remote that their currency was never quoted in *The Times* and I could never discover what the jobs were worth. I applied for Extension lecturing. I gave a sample lecture, in some Fenland village, to a large yawning dean and six gloomy workers, and much to my surprise – for the lecture hadn't been good and the dean didn't like me – I was accepted. A few weeks later I was told I could begin my Extension work, in autumn, on what seemed to me far too big a slice of North Devon. But just before the summer term ended, I dismissed all thought of regular employment – a decision received with bitter incredulity at home in Bradford – and decided to freelance in London. I had a wife, and might soon have a child, and our total capital was exactly fifty pounds.

Nowadays I often see advertisements showing very young men, younger than I was in 1922, staring dubiously at personnel managers and saying: 'Does this position carry a pension?' But let me add that I do not believe in these young men who are looking forward to pensions, to a comfortable descent into the grave, before they have even started work. I suspect they belong to the mythical world of advertisement, in which whole families are radiant at the thought of a new cake-mix or laxative. (Politicians are now half in that world, only half in ours.) It is my belief that no crackpot scheme could be devised, no matter what discomforts and dangers it might offer nor how doubtful and irregular its pay might be, that would not draw a queue of young men to chance it, especially young men recovering from our highest forms of education: *Have honours degree, will travel.* So I am merely recording a fact, not playing the old boasting role of the self-made man, when I mention this jobless journey to London.

It was easier for a young writer in the early Twenties to earn a living than it is today. But this statement needs some qualification. There is actually more money to be made now, with films and TV and radio, but to make it the young writer risks walking into a trap. Once trapped, probably already spending more than taxation allows him to spend, he finds it increasingly difficult even to begin doing the work he originally set out to do. (This may explain the scarcity of large-scale writing in post-war Britain. America does better because it has so many grants, awards, fellowships.) My own generation, what was left of it, was luckier because we could pay our way writing reviews, critical and general essays, articles of every kind, short stories, for all of which there was ten times the space there is today. We were not compelled to turn ourselves into the kind of writer we had never wanted to be. Moreover, in terms of what money would buy, payment for the same sort of literary and journalistic work was much better then. I could produce comparative figures, but they would only alienate those readers who feel that authors should be outside economics, feeding on honeydew and drinking the milk of paradise. As it was, not only did I earn a living but, by doing two men's work, writing day and night, I was able to cope financially, if not emotionally, with my wife's long and fatal illness.

I had some help when I first arrived in London. Most of it came from J. C. Squire, an important figure then in literary journalism. I had met Squire at Cambridge, through my friend the poet Edward Davison (now Director of Studies at Hunter College, New York, and still my friend). I can just remember flatly contradicting Squire about ninety seconds after we had been introduced. This may have impressed him, though I doubt it. He may have seen in me a potential critic and essayist, Johnsonian in rigour, but what chiefly moved him, I think, to set me writing for his *London Mercury*, to mention me to various literary editors and publishers, to ask me to his house, where I probably looked even less at home than I felt, was the conviction that he ought to help an ex-infantryman.

This help from Squire, given when it was most needed, I deeply appreciated. I tried to express my gratitude in various ways, right down to the time when A. D. Peters, my agent and friend, and I organised a seventieth-birthday dinner for him. But ours was an embarrassing relationship. The truth is, Squire and I never really liked each other. There was no active dislike between us, but we didn't enjoy each other's company. I can imagine many reasons why he could not enjoy mine. I thought his talk contained too many large statements impossible to believe. It lacked the basic honesty on which friendship is built. He began as a Socialist rebel and ended a High Tory, but this regression was simply so many changes of attitude.

Squire had astonishing natural gifts as a writer. He was far more richly endowed than the people who soon began to sneer at him. But through some flaw of character he could not put his gifts to the best use. (When we are young we think genius or talent is everything; later we discover how much depends on character.) Except for a few longish poems, solemn exercises in versification, everything he did was done at the last

moment, rushed to the printer with the ink still wet. Given
these circumstances, he performed some astounding feats of
composition. He could write verses, critical essays, reviews,
during the time it took most other men to read through what
they had written. But cold print makes no allowance for such
circumstances. Though he had a wide knowledge of literature,
from the Twenties.onwards I suspect he cared more about
architecture and cricket. His cricket side, the Invalids, was a
Marx Brothers film in white flannels. It can be found, in
cracking form, in Archie MacDonell's *England, Their
England*. Squire was soon denounced as a literary dictator of
belated Edwardian tastes, but to those of us who knew him
better he was something more rewarding – a comic character.

It was Squire who sent me along to Robert Lynd, who was
literary editor of the *Daily News*, for which I did a lot of reviewing. Lynd was a fine critic and essayist, but he was entirely
without ambition, was content to write short pieces as and
when they were required, free from the solitary hard labour
that books of any size demand. He was an enchanting character,
and in his company, for more than twenty-five years, I 'fleeted
the time carelessly as they did in the golden world' : the hours
were full of good talk – once your ear was attuned to his Irish
mutter – and flavoured with whisky. Of all the scores and
scores of writers I have known, I think Lynd and Walter de la
Mare were the most delightful characters and companions.
(During those first years in London I used to go out to de la
Mare's house at Anerley to play charades. I would probably
go and play charades even now, if anybody asked me to; but
nobody does: we are all too busy having-it-so-good.) This is
not the lavish testimonial it may appear to be; indeed, Lynd
and de la Mare deserve higher praise. Writers rarely make
good company. Mostly they give out too little and are too self-
absorbed. If they feel they are not doing well, they are over-

critical and bitter. If the world is taking them seriously, then they take themselves even more seriously, becoming complacent and pompous, like politicians. Authorship is a demanding and unhealthy occupation. You sit alone for long hours, spinning the stuff out like a spider. Creation may be all very fine, but getting it down on paper is a hard task. Painters and sculptors with their clutter of materials and gadgets have more fun in working hours, and are livelier companions out of them. Those actors who can forget the Theatre for an hour or two are better company than most writers. So are musicians, so long as they are not conductors who think they are more important than Beethoven. All this is a warning to those readers – there must be still a few left – who wonder how to meet the writers they admire: they are in search of disappointment.

It was Squire too who recommended me to the publisher John Lane, whose firm, the Bodley Head, was in need of a reader. (Readers and dustmen then; 'literary advisers' and 'garbage disposal officers' now.) I spent one morning a week in Vigo Street, deciding what was worth reading and reporting on, throwing out the thousand-page history of Jerusalem in blank verse or the reminiscences of a busy life in Stockport. The rest of the work was done at home, after I had finished my own writing for the day. I was paid six pounds a week, a useful regular income in 1923, when seven-course dinners were to be had in Soho for half-a-crown. Although I did this publisher's reading quickly and impatiently I cannot remember turning down any manuscript that became later, in other publishers' hands, an important book, and I recommended the first novels of Graham Greene and C. S. Forester among others. (Some of these novelists, however, Graham Greene leading them, went elsewhere.) A few of my discoveries flopped. The one I most regretted was an elaborate and deeply subjective story about children, *Cubwood*, to which Walter de la Mare wrote an

introduction. It is an odd book, and its author, Sunderland
Lewis, was himself an oddity, a fantastic elderly man who had
toiled for years writing about these children. He used to arrive
in Vigo Street, always muffled in scarves, bringing further
batches of manuscript, though the story was already far too
long and involved and gave us enormous trouble cutting and
trimming it for publication. After nearly forty years it might
be worth reprinting, perhaps as a paperback. We could do with
one that de la Mare could praise.

When I first met him, John Lane must have been only a year
or two older than I am now. He seemed to me ancient: small
and bearded, puckered and peering – his sight was so bad he
could no longer read. His talk and manner contrived to suggest
a retired diplomat or a connoisseur who had run through a
fortune, and not at all a hard bargainer in the book trade. In fact
this symbolic figure of the Nineties was the son of a Devon
yeoman and came up to London to be a railway clerk, which he
was for eighteen years. How many leading publishers today
began as railway clerks? Don't we deceive ourselves when we
imagine that our society now is more open and widely inviting,
more alight with opportunity, than that of eighty years ago?
But I am thinking now of matters I understand, not of property
deals, advertising, commercial television, bank robberies.

John Lane had conjured an extraordinary career out of his
clerk's top hat, but at the time I began to read for him he must
have felt his particular world had vanished – that small but
influential world, half-aesthetic, half-smart, in which the
cleverer ladies, coping with luncheon parties, cooed and trilled
over the latest Bodley Head volume and the current number of
The Yellow Book. Had he been younger he might have realised
that the spirit of the early Twenties was in fact closer to that of
his own Nineties, not in all but in most respects, than either of
them was to the spirit of the period between, beginning about

1898 and ending somewhere among the ruins of the war. However, nothing had changed his publisher's technique. After a superb meal at the Café Royal, preferably when a second liqueur brandy had been accepted, there would be a slight shift in his manner, urbane but seignorial. Out of his pocket would come a contract, originally designed to keep poets in garrets – thirteen copies to count as twelve, a possible rise from 10% to 12½% royalty after 10,000 had been sold, first refusal of the next four books, and an advance of £50 – hm, well – even £75. But he was a good host and had many fascinating anecdotes: it was like lunching with literary history.

I wrote reviews and critical articles for the *London Mercury*, the *Bookman*, the *Spectator*, *Saturday Review*, *Outlook*, *Daily News*, *Daily Chronicle*, and some others, including two monthlies, one American and the other Swedish, whose names I have forgotten. Apart from writing a long leading article on Peacock for *The Times Literary Supplement*, I stayed away from editorial offices where reviewing and criticism were anonymous. I can see no justification for unsigned reviews. (We do not know even now, I believe, whether it was Lockhart or Croker who was so stupid and malicious in the *Quarterly* about Tennyson's *Poems* of 1832.) They encourage dirty work, what Philip Guedalla called the 'stealthy assassins'. Embittered dons lurk in those thickets, knife in hand. Now and again I was unfair to older novelists like Arnold Bennett, but I never undertook a hatchet job for a literary editor, nor ever asked specially for a book so that I could slash it. When I have done regular book columns, in which I could choose what I wanted to review, I have always kept silent about books that I entirely disliked. Literary editors who encourage cut-throat reviews, because they are easy to do and make lively reading, are working for the wrong sort of paper: they should drop the 'literary' and try the other side of Fleet Street. And journalists with a talent for vituperation should not waste it on comparatively harmless novels, poems, volumes of essays; they should take a look at public life.

One thing that was wrong with literary editing thirty-five years ago has not been put right even now. This is the ridiculously small proportion of space allotted to reviews of fiction. Any routine biography or dim volume of memoirs may be given far more attention than a new novel that might be a work of genius. We suffer still from the nineteenth-century notion that writing or reading novels is a frivolous occupation, all right for women but unworthy of solid men. To this day we hear these men say: 'No, hardly ever look at a novel – prefer something more substantial.' By which they usually mean *My Years on Safari* and *Famous Mistresses of the French Court*.

It was difficult then, as it is today, for a young English writer to attempt anything ambitious in criticism. It was impossible for me, with two young children and hospital bills mounting up. I did some odds and ends of books somewhere on the edge of criticism proper, one on *English Humour* and another on the *English Comic Characters*. Both Ralph Richardson and Charles Laughton, when I first met them, told me how much time they had spent with my *Comic Characters*, though I find it hard to believe the book could have been of much professional help to these fine actors. I was able to write two volumes in the *English Men of Letters* series, because Macmillans commissioned them. (I remember discussing one of them in the office with a certain Harold Macmillan.) One was on Peacock, the other on his son-in-law, George Meredith. The latter, once a demigod of the intellectuals, had fallen entirely out of fashion, and was – as he still is – either ignored or shockingly undervalued.

For most of Meredith's work I was an enthusiastic though

not uncritical advocate. But when I came to consider his life, reading every anecdote I could find and listening to a few people who had known him, the more I learnt about him the less I liked him as a man. I could not escape the impression that he was affected, conceited, and cold-hearted. Possibly the anecdotes I read and heard – I remember some of them came from Violet Hunt, who had known him when she was a girl – were misleading, for we are not simply the sum total of the stories told about us; but I had to use what evidence I could find. Years after my book appeared, Barrie, who worshipped Meredith, told me he had never dared to read it, he was so much afraid of what I might have written. Just after publication I had an angry letter from Will Meredith, the novelist's son, together with a number of references to my book, challenging its opinions, not its facts. The irony of this is that George Meredith's unsympathetic treatment of his sons had helped to feed my prejudice against the great man. Possibly I had been wrong, but it is also possible that by the time he wrote to me Will Meredith had a strong vested interest in his father.

It is worth recalling how I began that book on Meredith, if only for the benefit of any very young writers in the audience. I was living then at Chinnor Hill, on the far edge of the Chilterns, but spending much time in London, going to and from Guy's Hospital. I got back to Chinnor Hill, late one afternoon, so deep in despair I did not know what to do with myself. I was nearly out of my mind with misery. Had I been close to a town I might have visited friends, gone to a pub or a cinema, wandered about the streets, but Chinnor Hill was miles from anywhere. Finally, just to pass the time while I was at the bottom of this pit, I decided to write something – anything –a few pages to be torn up after I felt less wretched. On my desk was a rough list of chapters for the Meredith book. I chose one of the chapters, not the first, and slowly, painfully, set to work on it. In an hour I was writing freely and well. It is in fact one of the best chapters in the book. And I wrote myself out of my misery, followed a trail of thought and words into daylight.

Notice – and now I address the aspirants in the audience – the subject was far removed from my own life; I didn't lighten my woes by describing them; both the release from anguish and the good work done came from the necessary concentration, the effort, the *act* of writing. Perhaps, as I have already suggested, it would be better not to be a writer, but if you must be one – then, I say, *write*. You feel dull, you have a headache, nobody loves you – *write*. It all seems hopeless, that famous 'inspiration' will not come – *write*. If you are a great genius, you will make your own rules; but if you are not – and the odds are heavily against it – go to your desk, no matter how high or low your mood, face the icy challenge of the paper – *write*. Sooner or later the goddess will recognise in this a devotional act, worthy of benison and grace. But if what I am saying seems nonsense, do not attempt to write for a living. Try elsewhere, making sure the position carries a pension.

2

The early essays I wrote, coming out in various periodicals and then in volume form in *Papers from Lilliput*, *I for One*, *Open House*, were mostly literary exercises. There was nothing much I really wanted to say, but for some years I took great pains with these pieces, like a man learning how to play an instrument. Though I kept right on into the Thirties writing weekly essays, first for the *Saturday Review*, while Gerald Barry edited it, and then moving with Barry to the *Week End Review*, short-lived but glorious, I knew that this kind of essay, personal in tone but elaborately composed, was already almost an anachronism. It had had an Indian summer in the period 1900–1914, when newspapers still published essays. Strong demand brought rich supply, as I believe it does in all the arts. If the English switched from football to chamber music, for example, they would soon have some masterpieces.

Already in the early Twenties the essay as a form had dropped behind the times, but, then, I was behind them too. Half of me was still living in the years 1910–14, when I was growing up and first trying to write. (One part of me, perhaps going down deepest, will always belong to these years.) The War, an incubator for some young men, had merely slowed me up. All Cambridge did was to give me a chance to read as widely and as long as I pleased. I got far more out of its second-hand bookshops than I did out of its lecture-rooms. I remember, for instance, buying a bargain lot of the old *Mermaid* dramatists, faded and spotted volumes (I have them still), and then shutting myself in, with plenty of tobacco and beer, to devour them all. I read everything except newspapers and journals of opinion, those with 'Aftermath' articles. (Political journalists could not forgo 'aftermath', just as chairmen still rarely escape from 'without more ado'.) I have been told I was blusteringly dogmatic in those days, but about what, I cannot imagine now. I know that I had few convictions, ideas, opinions. I was really a junior wool clerk of 1913, let loose among books and beginning to learn how to write. For the pay-off, as film men say, I had to wait nearly forty years, when at last I could write *Literature and Western Man*.

I dropped even further behind the times, in the London where I collected my review copies, because literary valuations and judgments were changing fast. I think I recognised this change even then, though only in its more superficial aspect. The journalist-critics I knew might still have the space and plenty of readers, but they were rapidly losing that all-important central influence, they were no longer capturing the intellectual young. They were too easy and good-humoured; they talked too much; they drank too much whisky. There was now arriving, to dominate the centre, a new kind of criticism, colder and harder, intolerant in manner, arrogant in tone, and so immediately attractive to intellectual youth, itself intolerant and arrogant. It was theological and absolutist: severe high priests moved in. Only a small amount of writing, written by and for an élite, was Literature, all else was rubbish. Few would be saved. It coldly rejected the idea, which my Twenties friends held and I still hold, that criticism should address itself to intelligent men and women of the world, asking for many different kinds of pleasure from many different kinds of books and authors. These new critics were like members of a grim little secret society, making out lists of the few who would be allowed to survive, the many who must be assassinated. As their influence grew, I was out-of-date before I even began.

On a deeper level there was a change that I did not perceive then but can understand now. The English idea of Literature – the capital letter is deliberate – at last caught up with the French. Modern Literature could be created only by the introvert, deep in his inner world. What was produced by the extrovert, facing the outer world, was simply so much popular entertainment, not Literature at all. And nobody need remind me that really great literature is both introverted and extroverted: I know it.

We can put it another way, without calling in depth psychology. With this change the qualities looked for and most highly regarded were originality, strangeness, and intensity. On the other hand, what no longer counted, except perhaps as signs of weakness, were breadth and vitality. (Thus, Fielding and Scott were now ignored, and so, until his later work was better understood, was Dickens.) If we set aside the unique, the truly great, we can divide writers of any importance into two classes. There are those who write out of their extra-ordinariness. They approach the world at a sharp angle. Creation for them is compensatory – for a wretched childhood, bad physique, weak sight, or some sexual deficiency. Line them up and it is as if a clinic had just been evacuated. Almost misfits themselves, they know compassion, though there still remains a vengeful element in their work. But it has originality, strangeness, intensity, what the modern movement demands. What it never has is something critics in that movement never ask for, never miss – affection.

Writers in the opposing class approach the world squarely, in this and other respects behaving like most ordinary men. Indeed, they write out of a heightened ordinariness. What distinguishes them from the common run is not some con-volution in their inner history; they simply happen to have sharper senses and wits, more energy and vitality, and enjoy using words. Look down the centuries of literature, as I had to do a few years ago, and you discover more writers of this kind than of the other. Take a short view and they seem to have vanished, as if literary history had turned a sharp corner, which indeed it did round about the time I first went to London. But are there signs now, after half a lifetime, of a turn the opposite way, from introversion and strangeness and intensity to extroversion and breadth and vitality? Is affection coming back from exile? The recent *Characters of Love* by John Bayley, one of the best of our younger critics, was most warmly received. In its Epilogue you can hear the tide turning.

Often we catch glimpses of authors only in the distorting mirrors held up by their critics and admirers. When I meet James Joyce in the solemn chapters of his American idolaters, he seems monstrous, so narrow, humourless, arrogant. But that is what an idol should be. Probably, tongue in cheek, he offered them what they had gone all the way to Paris to find. In the reminiscences of his friends, Mary and Padraic Colum, we discover a very different character. So did I, the only time I spent an evening in his company. He was all amiability, and sang, in a pleasant light tenor, many comic songs. Probably it is too difficult to sing comic songs to pilgrims from American Eng. Lit. departments.

Being in the trade, if only as an apprentice, I met many authors from the early Twenties onwards. I began by sharing the same party roof or bar counter with them, not seeking them out at home. I was too proud and shy to present myself at the front doors of genius, and now I am sorry. I never set eyes on Hardy, though I had two letters from him. Conrad was still alive, and for a talk with him I might have risked a snub; but I was warned he was a sick man. Yeats was my favourite contemporary poet. I heard him read his poems – he had a deep-toned incantatory manner that improved his early work but was not quite right for his later and better poems – but, though we had many friends and acquaintances in common, I never spent five minutes alone with him. However, it might not have worked out. Gogarty said to me in Dublin: 'Yeats is now so aristocratic, he's evicting imaginary tenants.'

That remark above about sharing the same party roof or bar counter was not fanciful. Most of my meetings with authors took place either in Fleet Street pubs, roughly between 11.30 and 2.30, or late in the evening at literary parties. I have not been near those pubs for years but I cannot believe they hear as much wit as they did in the early Twenties. Some of the best talk came from men who are almost forgotten now: G. H. Mair, for example, who was thought to be the brightest young man in the country when he left Oxford to join the staff of the

Manchester Guardian. (When asked afterwards if Mair was a careful writer, James Bone, London editor of the paper, replied: 'He cabled a semicolon from Moscow.') But he talked too much, drank too much. Though only in his late thirties when I knew him, he seemed already a shaky elderly man, dowsing the last glimmer of ambition in – of all things – cheap pub port. But his talk, even then, sparkled with unrehearsed wit. Not much of it spilled over into print perhaps, yet Fleet Street still had some touches of quality, provided by such ruined characters.

These pubs were not quiet and often it was hard to hear what was being said. I have spent hours standing with Robert Lynd, H. M. Tomlinson, James Bone, trying to understand what they were muttering and murmuring in their respective Belfast, Cockney, Glasgow accents, never catching more than a word or two. Tomlinson, who looked like a battered elf, must have been bringing out his *Tidemarks* about then. I thought it a masterpiece of travel literature, and have never changed my mind. There are some books that writers should keep close by them, to restore faith in their craft of prose when they are feeling jaded. *Tidemarks* seems to me one of those books – a pen-sharpener.

Belloc often came marching in, wearing an Inverness-cape overcoat and a John Bull type of hat. He was a formidable man and many people were afraid of him, but I always found him courteous, charming, and free of any condescension towards the young. As he was descended from Joseph Priestley, he insisted upon maintaining, even though I made no claims myself upon the great Joseph, that he and I were related. He was not only an enormous character, a complete original – imagine him talking on television! – but he also had an astonishing variety of talents. If he is mostly remembered now in Catholic circles – though while he did much for them, they

did precious little for him – that is chiefly because of something he could not help, his birth. He was not only half-English,
half-French, he was half very English, half very French, each
side pulling away from the other. It is this division that makes
him seem so often over-mannered, histrionic, not quite real.
Though he was still only in his forties when the First War
ended, he belonged essentially, one felt, to that world of jolly
debate which vanished in 1914.

Chesterton was four years younger than Belloc, but he too
seemed to belong to an age that had gone. For all his bulk, there
was something ghostly about him. Although I saw him only a
few times in the pubs, where he called for no stoups and
flagons but sipped a ginger ale, I did meet him elsewhere on
several occasions. I may have been unlucky every time, but
certainly, though pleasant enough, he was anything but jovial
and high-spirited, usually appearing tired and unresilient, man
half-alive. After all I had read about him before 1914, he was a
disappointment. Possibly the serious illness he had had, early
in the War, had changed him. I find the same difference in his
writing, for to my mind all the best of it, in which he is really
enjoying intellectual high jinks, was done before 1914. He will
be remembered as a young man writing for young men,
against a background of long golden Edwardian afternoons.

However raw he may be, a young man can hold his own in a
pub. At large evening parties, wearing dress clothes that are a
poor fit, meeting the bright ironical glances of the women, he
will be far less sure of himself, unable to decide whether to
drink little and play safe or to swallow everything offered and
let rip. (Usually I chose the first and then soon switched to the
second.) I was never a constant party-goer, for I was not
always living in London and anyhow I often worked late into
the night. Nevertheless, at the parties I did attend, right from
the first, literary London came to life for me in a way, I

imagine, it no longer does for young writers. Ours, I suspect, is increasingly a more solitary and sourer profession, a rat-race without even a sight of the other rats. Before Dickens sailed for America the second time, at the end of 1867, he was given a colossal public banquet; even before I set out early in 1931, for my first visit, Heinemann's gave me what they called 'a Columbus Party'; but what is a popular writer given now? Probably a couple of paragraphs by gossip-writers and a brief idiotic appearance on television.

Nothing is lost and much can be gained when writers of all ages, newcomers and old hands, the famous and the unknown, help one another to drinks and sandwiches. It should be late in the evening, though: they ought to be working at cocktail-party time, and, even if they are not, they will get nothing out of a cocktail party except noise, a spoilt appetite, and probably a headache. Young writers can discover later at night that their elders are not necessarily pompous old mandarins. Ageing authors, let us hope, may realise that the young are not simply wild and silly. Writers may not be the best company, as I have already suggested, but there is such a thing as a pro-fessional bond, not to be despised in a country that barely tolerates writers who are still alive. It has been said that criticism suffers where there is any wide acquaintance with authors. I do not agree. If criticism is worth anything at all, then acquaintance improves it. A writer's look, his tone of voice, his manner in company, a chance remark, may offer a critic the clue he needs. Finally, it is all too easy for a young writer, as he toils on and on alone, deep in his own world, to begin to feel that what he is doing is shadowy, unreal, a laborious nonsense. If he meets other writers, then he finds himself with men and women, now smiling, who have also known and have escaped from that treacherous dream.

Not long ago I learnt indirectly that I was accused of 'not

wanting to meet the young playwrights'. This seemed to me outrageous. I have never been asked to meet these young playwrights. I know no plan of hospitality, no organisation, no social machinery, that would bring us together. If any host and hostess entertain the young playwrights, then they must have forgotten my existence. But why don't I entertain them myself? Am I too mean or too shy? Neither, I hope. But I am a realist – I have more than once been described as an idealist, but this is quite wrong – and as a realist I know this plan would not work. We should all be too solemn or nervous, or both, and feel fatuous. We need a roof that belongs to none of us, and, beneath it, a pleasant social occasion.

Years ago I used to be a member of a playwrights' club, meeting once a month for lunch. I was present when Barrie, after the death of Pinero, accepted the presidency of this club. He made a little speech, delivered in his usual muffled voice, as if he were talking through a plaid. But Barrie was a master of timing, and of an artful counterpoint of short phrases, cigar-puffs and coughs. Looking like a ravaged troll, he said: 'When I used to come to this club' – *puff*, *puff* – 'many years ago' – *puff* – 'one man was always here' – *cough* – 'an Irishman with a red beard who never stopped talking.' He paused, timing it to a fraction of a second; then added dreamily, wistfully: 'I've often wondered what became of him.'

Barrie was not to be found at parties. I made his acquaintance after he had written to me, at some length, about various books of mine – a friendly practice of his generation. To see him I had to ascend, slowly and creakily in an antique lift, to that flat of his high up in Adelphi Terrace, where he must have had the most wonderful view in London. Later, the building across the way was pulled down, and where it had been there was a hole with a mechanical excavator at work. He pointed to it, one afternoon, and said that at dusk, when the workmen had all gone, this machine would creep out, to grab a few more giant mouthfuls of earth. At such moments, as you stared at that melancholy ruin of a face, listened to that weary choked-up voice, you were ready to believe anything he told you. Both in Adelphi Terrace and my own house – then, in the Thirties, 3 The Grove, Highgate Village, where Coleridge lived and died – he played with my children, who acted up nobly, because in fact, as they confided to me, he frightened them. Here they showed more perception than all the young men who sneered at Barrie. He could of course be distressingly whimsical and mawkish, chiefly, I think, because, remembering the audiences with whom he was a favourite, he forced these passages. He was a Scot tickling a tear and a smile out of the English upper-middle classes. But what was native to him – and now forget *Peter Pan* and remember grim little masterpieces like *The Will* and *Farewell, Miss Julie Logan* – was very un-English, belonging to a melancholy and eerie inner world. Like all good Scots writers, and unlike all the English, he was haunted by the devil. If his work, the best of it technically superb and full of strange symbolism, has ever been properly examined, then there is a good book I have missed. He was an odd companion. He created huge silences, tarns into which any remarks prompted by your social conscience fell and vanished like tossed pebbles. I think I got by because I smoked a pipe as large as his, so that we puffed away companionably, like two engines in a siding.

3

The great panjandrums of those early literary parties were Shaw, Wells, and Arnold Bennett. At first I could hardly believe I was in the same room with them. This does not mean I was unusually naïve or much given to veneration. The circumstances of the time must be remembered and understood. In the years immediately before the First War – those of war-time itself hardly count – not only had I read eagerly their own work but every day or so I had read *about* them. In those days, before film stars and 'television personalities' (God save us) and mysterious gossip-column pets hogged the popular press, writers like Shaw, Wells, Bennett, were *news*, daily journalism's stand-by. (Even as late as the Twenties Bennett could declare – foolishly, in my opinion – that a successful novelist should be mentioned in one newspaper or another every day.) With no publicity departments working for them, their doings and sayings were reported, week in and week out. Even people who never read a word they wrote knew all about them. This might have been good for literature or bad for it – I am not debating this question, merely recording facts. During my Swan Arcadian time in Bradford, Shaw, Wells and Bennett moved through the national scene like those big heads on stilts in carnival processions. And after all, behind them was achievement, good work done for ever. Why shouldn't I have been impressed?

Though we exchanged a certain amount of hospitality, Shaw and I were never more than amiable acquaintances. Probably the gap of years was too wide. If he had to ignore nearly forty of them, then he wanted either a disciple or an audience. Discipleship was not for me, so I remained on the audience level. The performance was often brilliant, always touched with an intensely personal charm not to be found in print or lines for actors. It was well for him that he had brought his voice – and a fine voice it was – from Dublin. If he had had a North Country accent, then probably not later than 1895 he would have been lynched. With that voice he got away with polemic murder. But a performance, however dazzling, is not an adequate substitute for an exchange of ideas and opinions.

After the first few encounters, having given genius and age their due, I like to say something too. (But Mrs Shaw was a good listener. God knows she had had plenty of practice.) Possibly I glowered at him as he went on and on – I have the opposite of a poker face, for mine expresses *more* than I am feeling – and that may be one reason why I was never one of his favourites, which included some rather rum members of my own generation. Although, until he reached extreme old age, a grimly ironic present to him after he had declared men did not live long enough, he knew what was being written or played in the Theatre, I suspect he saw no point in younger writers existing at all, especially if they wrote plays. The world had G.B.S. – why not leave it at that?

During the time I knew him, when he was of course from the first an old man, I think he was happiest at the Malvern Drama Festival, of which he was the central figure. It was organised by Barry Jackson, who had enthusiasm, intelligence *and* money. Without his backing, Shaw's later plays would probably have never reached the London stage at all. At Malvern, crammed with his admirers, G.B.S. could show off like mad. I once saw him do some clowning, for an amateur film-maker, that all the money in Hollywood could not have bought. Wearing a Norfolk jacket and knickerbockers, he hurried to and from the Festival Theatre or went striding up the Beacon. I thought once of engaging about half-a-dozen six-foot character actors and giving them white beards, Norfolk jackets and knickerbockers, so that next day there would seem to be a G.B.S. down every street in Malvern. How angry he would have been! And what a pleasant little festival that was, thirty years ago! True, the playhouse itself was badly ventilated, so that after spending high summer days up on the Beacon, I have slept through centuries of English Drama there, from *Gammer Gurton's Needle* to *London Assurance*. But the town was the right size, being small and compact, easily creating an intimate atmosphere. What Edinburgh offers us is not a festival, in the sense in which I understand that term, but a large crowded city suddenly bursting with culture, a bewildering Barnum and Bailey's show of symphonic music, opera and drama, with the intimacy of Waterloo Station on a Bank Holiday.

I remember one very odd encounter with Shaw. I was spending the winter in Arizona, and was making one of many visits to the Grand Canyon. I think it was the time when we went down the Canyon and stayed at the lodge on the floor of it, far below the rim, in another climate. But there, on the south rim, was Shaw, who had arrived with a world-cruise party from the Pacific coast. He was peevish. He refused to wonder and exclaim at the Grand Canyon, muttering something about Cheddar Gorge. The truth was, I am afraid, that he was determinedly resisting the spell of this marvel, at once awe-inspiring and beautiful, the most ego-shrinking of all earth's spectacles. It is only fair, however, to add that he was then about eighty and had probably been travelling too long and seeing too many sights.

Like many persistent mockers, Shaw had to laugh before anybody else did. His mockery was partly defensive, like the beard he grew, the boxing he learnt, the pose he adopted of being bored with sex. That he was a man of genius only a fool would deny; he was a man of genius who was also practical, sensible and kind; but there was a tricky element in him, a want of complete intellectual honesty, the result perhaps of his having built up a persona as finished and hard as a carapace. Clamped inside it, speaking through a megaphone, he was tricky about sex, about dictators, about equality, about Russia, where he would not have lasted a month except as a distinguished visitor.

How my elders and betters could be fooled by the dictators!
Once, over a dining table in the later Thirties, I dared to argue
against both Shaw *and* Wells, who were declaring that
Mussolini was a very great man, far greater than Napoleon. I
maintained with some noise and heat that he was in fact, as
time would prove, a blown-up mountebank. Why had
Mussolini taken them in? Was it simply because they had been
to his Italy and had been given the special treatment dictator-
ships reserve for visiting celebrities? I think not. Shaw and
Wells, both of them passionately concerned with public
affairs, had lived in England too long. It was not too bad before
the First War, when Asquith's Government was in power and
prominent writers, however scathing their criticism might be,
were not completely shut out from political life. But by the
Thirties, if you were not in politics, almost unable to think
about anything else, then you had better mind your own
business. So, feeling powerless, helpless, just another pair of
spectators in the stand, they relieved their resentment by
over-praising a Mussolini. I couldn't blame them, even
though I challenged everything they said about that black-
shirted bullfrog.

Shaw and Wells, however, had really very little in common.
In many respects they were opposites. With Wells, I think, I
enjoyed as much friendship as great fame and seniority, nearly
thirty years, could possibly allow. Though irritable, with a
lightning detonator and a full charge of explosive, he was one
of the friendliest of men. He had never bothered about a
persona. He was with you, not performing at you. In any
company he thought aloud; and many of his books are simply
this excited thinking aloud. If he couldn't stand up to Shaw in
debate, that was because his emotions were involved and
Shaw's weren't. Of all the English writers I have known, he
was the most honest, the frankest, the one least afraid of telling

the truth. If he often offended public opinion, that is chiefly because English public opinion feeds itself with cant and humbug. He had not more dirty linen than most other authors, but, with a kind of innocence, he did his laundry work in the open. His genius was entirely literary, not scientific, but his early training, his discovery of a wide rich world through science, gave him permanently the air of a man making some hasty last-minute experiments in a lab. He was an artist gasping for breath in a scientific climate.

His indifference to literary reputation was not a pose. He meant it when he said that he thought of himself as a kind of journalist. After the First War, he became world-famous as a popular educator, a light in dark continents. This was not understood in London, where he was thought to be fading away rather noisily. He never behaved like a sensible man of letters, for he hopped from publisher to publisher so that no one house had a continuing interest in his work. But though he might pretend not to care about literature, for which there would be time when the world was saved, actually he read a lot of new books and was always glad to meet young authors. He never remained aloof or condescended. I remember attending a party given by F. N. Doubleday, the American publisher. His star author was Kipling. And Kipling was there at the party but not with it, for the whole time he stayed in an anteroom, talking to Doubleday and glowering through the doorway at the rest of us. Now if Wells had been at the party, he would have been in the middle of it, the life of it, not projecting a death-wish on to it from the next room. It is true that Wells was always writing in a rage because the 2000 million people in the world could not instantly agree to work together, and yet was himself capable of wrecking a committee of six within an hour. But at least he knew this – he wrote with perception and wisdom about the irritability in private of men who could make sacrifices for the public good – and could be candid about it and laugh at himself. His talk, all in that squeaky voice which was almost intolerable coming from a platform, was wonderfully far-ranging, rich in meat and fun, glittering with a malice that had no real harm in it. He escaped both the pompous complacency of the successful author and the dull caution of the scientist, making the best of both his worlds. He was, what is surely rare, a great figure who could exist in a sort of family atmosphere of cheerful indulgence, give-and-take, affection.

Perhaps the strangest day I ever spent was one in August 1946. I was directing a comedy of mine, a box of little experimental tricks called *Ever Since Paradise*, later very successful abroad, from Stockholm down to Madrid, perhaps because I was not directing it. Before the play went out on a twelve-week pre-London tour, we were having a full dress rehearsal, with all the quick scene-and-lighting changes, at the Scala Theatre. Postponement was impossible. But Wells had just died, and I had been asked to conduct the cremation service at Golders Green. Therefore I had to fit this service into the dress rehearsal. As soon as the first act was over and I had given the necessary notes, I had to rush up to Golders Green and somehow take over this funeral service, without the familiar ritual and language that cushions us against grief. Then, with no break but the car-journey, back I went to the second act of the comedy. Yet I was perhaps the luckiest there in that funeral chapel, for this was no routine mourning: it was dear old H.G. who had gone; so it was better to have something else that had to be done at once. And how, if he had known, he would have grinned and chuckled! I can hear that high-pitched croak of his, beginning: 'Yers – yers – Priestley – busy man – pretending to be a parson one minute – then, next minute, messing about with the silly old stage – yers——'

The third of the trio, Arnold Bennett, I met on many occasions, but we were never friends. He was, I know, a friendly man, a lovable character to those who knew him well, and if it was my fault that there was constraint, tinged with hostility, between us, then I am sorry, and indeed was sorry from the moment – it was in March 1931 and I was staring at Tahiti – when the news of his death came over the ship's radio. The trouble was, I think, that there were always other people around when we met. We would have done better without an audience. The very last time we spoke we found ourselves moving out of the Queen's Hall together, after a Toscanini concert. 'Gives you——' Bennett jerked out, referring to the music, 'a lift – doesn't it?' There is a lot of him in that brief remark. He had responded eagerly to the music, but was determined not to sound high-flown about it. And the medicinal flavour of 'gives you a lift' was characteristic.

Once he acted as a referee for me. This is worth mentioning, if only for the sake of younger professional people who may find themselves involved in a dispute. I had had a sharp disagreement with my American publishers about the interpretation of a certain clause in the contract I had with them. They wouldn't budge; neither would I. If we had gone to law, the waste of time, nervous energy and money would have been appalling. We agreed to ask Bennett to act as referee and to accept without further argument his decision. Afterwards I sent him a noble box of cigars, and I still have somewhere his note of thanks, solemnly approving my taste in Havana tobacco. To writers and other people in the arts, when they are not trying to defend themselves against crooks, I recommend this practice of appointing a private referee, even if he is no Arnold Bennett. I think I would risk anybody's judgment rather than go to law.

Not that Bennett was the sagacious man of the world he

pretended to be. Perhaps only a man naïve at heart would make such a pretence. His life was full of ironies, some droll, some melancholy. Dorothy Cheston Bennett, in her reminiscences of him, has described how, when he was paying court to her in Paris, he would bring her a bunch of flowers every morning, and how these flowers were never quite fresh but about to fade, the keenly observant man-of-the-world novelist having been tricked each morning by the saleswomen. He wrote and talked more about money than most authors do, yet botched his own finances. He took elaborate care of himself and was fussy about trifles, yet contracted a fatal sickness because he ignored an obvious precaution – dying of typhoid fever, probably for no other reason than that he always insisted that water in France was safe to drink. He planned his career as few other writers have done, yet no sooner had his plan succeeded than everything began to go wrong. He had the capacity to enjoy a quiet bourgeois existence – cups of tea, an occasional water-colour, strumming on the piano, a cigar and a book – yet wasted time and energy, gave himself headaches and insomnia, because he felt he ought to live the life of a smart West End character. It was this 'smart' element in Bennett's later life that was wrong. Leading a gossip-column existence was tiring for the man and unrewarding for the novelist. We like him best in his last journals when, not bothering about being in the swim, he pops down the road to spend an hour in a tea-shop. Newspaper proprietors and millionaires made him dizzy; looking at ordinary people, going in and out of tea-shops, he was sympathetic, wise, compassionate. Now, when it is thirty years too late, I am sorry he must have thought me a bumptious and aggressive young man, altogether too pleased with himself. At heart I was not, just as he was not the strutting cad he appears to be in certain memoirs, especially those coming out of Bloomsbury, which, when he arrives on the scene, seem to me more caddish than he ever was. Though he is still out of fashion, as Trollope was for nearly half-a-century after his death, he may in the end outlast some fancier reputations.

That I saw something, if not very much, of John Galsworthy was chiefly due to the fact that we were both published by Heinemann. It was Charles Evans of Heinemann who probably brought Galsworthy the O.M. and the Nobel Prize, for it was he who thought of reprinting several Galsworthy novels in one volume and calling it *The Forsyte Saga*. It was no more a saga than its author was a Norse pirate, but immediately it sent Galsworthy's sales, which had been modest, shooting up, and established him abroad as the representative English novelist, a role he filled with handsome dignity. (But I think his most original work is to be found in his earlier plays.) He still enjoys this reputation in some distant circles. Not long ago I was asked to write something that English teachers in America could use in their schools, and the only passage I was implored afterwards to modify was one dealing with Galsworthy, so beloved by these teachers, I was told, that any adverse criticism would leave them shocked, resentful. I was never invited to stay in his country house, and was not sorry, because I was told it was filled with dogs. I can get along with a dog or two as well as the next man, but in any house where half-a-dozen of them are for ever asking to be let in or let out, genuine talk is not possible. I remember dining with him in Hampstead and then finding myself a member of the P.E.N. Club, largely because I had had so much to drink – no rough stuff with whisky bottles but a stately procession from dry sherry to port and brandy – that I would have scrawled a signature to anything. We met too on publishing occasions. He was always courteous and considerate but never seemed to me quite real. I think of him as a presence not as a person. No doubt Jack Galsworthy was somewhere there, but Jack Priestley had turned up too late to find him.

Among the established novelists who were all about ten years senior to me, the one I knew best was Hugh Walpole. We were close friends, especially in the later Twenties and earlier Thirties. We collaborated in a novel of sorts called *Farthing Hall*. The story was told in letters exchanged between a middle-aged scholar and an enthusiastic young man. Though I was neither middle-aged nor a scholar, this was the role I preferred, leaving eager youth and romance to Walpole. Possibly there is not much to be said in favour of this device as a literary form, but it made collaboration easy between two busy men with a couple of hundred miles separating them. In his remarkably skilful biography of Walpole, Rupert Hart-Davis writes: 'The object of the enterprise was to provide Priestley (whose share of the advance royalties, thanks to Hugh's name, would be substantial) with enough freedom and leisure to write the long novel he was planning.' This is quite true, and he could have added that the first suggestion came from Walpole, who had nothing to gain from such a colla-boration. The novel itself I have forgotten – it is more than thirty years since I looked at it – but not the act of kindness.

No doubt the creation of literature is more important than acts of kindness, but many of the people who have sneered at Walpole are not capable of either. He was a popular story-teller, not the great novelist he hoped he might be, but not only were the loudest jeerers not great novelists, they were not even popular story-tellers. There are always exceptions, and the principal one here was Somerset Maugham, whose Alroy Kear in *Cakes and Ale*, a character on which literary London pounced with glee, was a caricature of the sillier side of Walpole. Maugham strongly denied this at the time, but years afterwards, in an introduction to a new American edition of the book, he confessed that he had had Walpole in mind. Just as a less fortunate woman novelist, against whose novel an appeal was made and an injunction granted, had had in mind the author of *Cakes and Ale*. Heigh-ho!

Actually Walpole and I had less in common than Maugham and he had. It was a friendship of opposites. He was always wildly anxious to please, whereas I have a talent, almost a genius, for displeasing all but those near to me. He was fond of making lists, of favourite people, books, experiences and so on, something I never did even as a schoolboy. He really enjoyed lecturing, whereas only an urgent cause or a great deal of money gets me on to a platform. Even more he enjoyed writing – novels, articles, letters, anything – sitting at some fine desk and watching his pen glide over the paper; and I, pecking away at an old typewriter, detest it. He loved to fill his diary for months and months ahead with engagements for lunch, tea, dinner, supper, something that looks to me like slavery. He was solemnly concerned about everything that was happening in the book world, what Smith had written about Brown, what Green had said about Jones at a party, why Robinson was changing his publisher, how Grey was selling in America. He kept an eye on a sort of stock market of literary reputations, where that novelists's shares were going up, this critic's going down. I listened to his reports with interest and amusement but couldn't take them seriously, not caring a rap who was in or out, up or down.

So far of course I have slanted this comparison entirely in my own favour. (We always do unless we guard against it.) Now I will add that Walpole's innocent warm vanity was better than my cooler conceit. He had far more genuine humility than I had. He was more considerate, more generous, much kinder than I have ever been. I am not thinking now about his more spectacular acts of generosity, such as the help he gave the *Heldentenor* Melchior. I am thinking about all the little acts of kindness that you discovered only if you knew him very well, all the visits to cantankerous old men or ailing old women whom most people had forgotten, all the dull jobs for which he could expect no praise. He may have been desperately anxious to succeed, but even so he was far less self-centred than most writers are. He ran to welcome new talent in all the arts. The list of writers he helped is like a roll-call of contemporary British authors. 'I don't think,' said Osbert Sitwell, speaking for us all, 'there was any younger writer of any worth who has not at one time or another received kindness of an active kind, and at a crucial moment, from Hugh.' And this was the man who could be described, in the nastiest obituary I have ever read in *The Times*, as 'not popular among his fellow-writers'. Out came the last of the stealthy assassins to knife the corpse.

There are people who hate anybody else's happiness. They sharpen their knives at once when they see a bright eye, a broadening smile. (Is that why I have always looked so gloomy in public?) Nobody has ever enjoyed being a successful popular novelist more than Hugh Walpole did. He was like a schoolboy who suddenly found himself in the England Test side. There was also something feminine in him that enabled him to see himself in the role, and to enjoy that too. But there were really three Walpoles. Behind the large pink smiling successful writer, on his way from a literary lunch to a rugger match, was a fearful and trembling neurotic, haunted by nightmares ever since he was a child, half a world away from his parents and bullied without mercy at a bad prep school. It is he who brings the dark menace, the stretched and twanging nerves, into the strongest of his tales, the work of his that was never over-praised and is now, when new fiction in this manner is so hard to find, so surprisingly ignored. Behind him again was the simple good human creature who might have been trapped on that neurotic level, taking to revenge and crime, but who struggled through, writing too much and too quickly when his imagination was not sharply focused, but emerging into the daylight to find friends, to enjoy books, pictures, music, to give what help he could to younger or less fortunate writers.

Often I laughed *at* him but more often still I laughed *with* him; he was a lively talker and had far more humour in private than his public appearances might suggest. He had known the authors I had missed and was full of stories about them – he had some droll reminiscences of Henry James, for example – stories that he could talk much better than he could write. A lot of odd things had happened to him – he had been an eye-witness of the Russian Revolution, for instance, and, staying with Siegfried Wagner, he had been sent on walks with a shabby and rather pathetic little man just out of gaol, one Adolf Hitler. Now and then he might be over-excited, almost hysterical, probably because his diabetes was not under control, but most of the time, in all sorts of places from Borrowdale to Southern California, he was uproariously good company. I knew him for sixteen years, and have missed him for twenty. He is rarely mentioned, possibly because literary England has now such ample stores of enthusiasm, kindness, friendship. And possibly not.

4

The collaboration with Walpole in *Farthing Hall* was not my first attempt at fiction. Already I had made two tentative approaches, in *Adam in Moonshine* and *Benighted*, best-known as a film under the book's American title, *The Old Dark House*. I was hesitant not simply because I was committed to do so many other things, though I was, so that *Benighted* had to be written late at night, on top of a day's hard work. I didn't see myself as a born novelist. Had I been, obviously I would have been writing novels from the first, nothing would have been allowed to stop me. But this was not a literary form in which I could work instinctively and at ease, as I had done in the essay, as I came to do in descriptive-cum-autobiographical books like *English Journey* and *Midnight on the Desert*, and as I discovered later, to my astonishment, I could do in the supposedly more difficult dramatic form. I enjoy the neglected little art of narrative, sheer story-telling, my own or anybody else's. I can cope with a scene, in the direct dramatic manner. It is easy for me to write those descriptive bridge passages that most novels demand. What I find hard and wearisome to do is precisely what the born novelist has not even to think about at all.

This is the trick of maintaining an even flow of narration, steadily moving on no matter how thick and rich it may be. If a man can do this instinctively – and, let me add, very few men can – then God intended him to be a novelist. It is a very rare gift, this ability to keep the whole scene on the move without jerks and breaks, as if you had to empty a tube of toothpaste by squeezing the stuff out in one unbroken ribbon. But I must be careful here. I am not saying that a writer who has this gift can claim to be a great novelist. He or she may not be great at all. On the other hand, there have been great novelists who never had this gift. For example, I believe that Thackeray had it and Dickens hadn't, although he had so much else that now he far outshines Thackeray. Tolstoy had it of course, and without it could never have written *War and Peace*: he is a master of unforced evenly-flowing narration. What I am saying is that this particular gift belongs to the born novelist, who will work easily, without having to worry about the changing scene, the steady passage of time, when he writes in this form. And it is not a gift I possess.

Here many critics will shrug away the whole discussion. They will feel it comes out of some old-fashioned notion of the novel. I think such critics are wrong. They are taking short views of fiction, possibly because they have never had to take long views of it. They have been unduly influenced, almost conditioned, by about twenty-five years of experiment, at the end of which there appeared to be no such thing as a novel, no such person as a novelist. Either a writer had genius and something original, unique, he wanted to say, or he hadn't, and that was that. But it is possible to sympathise with and appreciate the experimenters, the form-changers, as I have always done, and yet sharply challenge this short view. The novel remains a particular form, though capable of many variations, and the novelist a particular kind of writer, capable of making the best use of that form. Certain standards and peculiar excellences still exist, just as government still exists after the smoke and dust of revolution have vanished.

Consider two men of original genius, Proust and Joyce. To my mind Proust was a born novelist, so superbly equipped for prose fiction that he would have excelled at it in any age. He gave the form a twist to suit his own particular purposes and temperament, nevertheless he is in the direct line of succession, what he is carrying forward is still the novel. This does not seem to me true of Joyce, whose rich comic genius I don't deny. Over and over again I have read that modern fiction really begins with Joyce, who opened a new road, led the way so that other writers could follow him, so on and so forth. No satisfactory evidence is produced to support these statements, and I do not believe a word of them. Where are all these novelists who owe so much to Joyce? (Even the deeply subjective method of narration had been attempted by others, notably

Dorothy Richardson, a brave if rather tedious originator.)
Wilful and whimsical, he did not give the form a twist but
proceeded to knock hell out of it, leaving it a dazzling ruin at
the end of a *cul-de-sac*. I doubt if he cared two sous what
happened to the novel. He was a man of genius but hardly a
novelist at all. Instead of being in the direct line, he stands
away from it, a monumental figure off the road, like one of the
colossi of Memnon.

The point, I trust, has been made. The novel is a continuing
though not unchanging form, and there are writers who are
essentially novelists just as there are others who are essentially
lyric poets. But much of the criticism in the weeklies and the
more influential reviewing in newspapers came to be done by
men who had lost all interest in prose fiction as such. They did
not want to read novels or write about them. If there was any
escape, they found it. Genius they could not ignore, but they
lifted it out of the stream of fiction, which they did ignore. The
result was that serious and influential critics and reviewers,
and probably a great many of their readers, cared nothing
about the progress of the novel. It belonged, if it did not reveal
genius, to women's library lists. Though it is in fact much
harder to write a moderately good novel of any size and
weight than it is to fill the same number of pages with critical
essays and reviews, an impression was created that a novelist
was an intellectual lightweight, a tea-time entertainer. I may
have been unlucky but I have never recognised any intellectual
giants among these critics and reviewers, and most of the good
or goodish novelists I have known have had wide interests and
lively minds.

Why, when I soon discovered I did not possess the born
novelist's gift I have already described, did I insist upon
writing fiction? It was not for lack of other work, for I had
plenty and was being reasonably well paid for it. Unless I was

lucky – and I never saw myself as a lucky type – financially I would be worse off, page by page, hour by hour. It was not easier work but harder, though eventually more exciting. I turned to fiction – and this also explains why I have attempted so many different things – because I had a lot of ideas that would not leave me in peace and because I could not resist the challenge. I had never really been encouraged to write anything – the West Riding, where I grew up, had a genius for discouragement as stony as its walls – and whenever I broke through, to be accepted as one kind of writer, I was given to understand that was about all I could do. I could write an essay but not a novel; I could write a novel but not a play; and because I wrote plays it did not follow I would know what to do with radio, the essential wartime medium; and so it went on. There was the challenge, time after time, and always I found it irresistible.

Restless, impatient, easily bored by any routine tasks, touchily independent but not really ambitious, mentally indolent except when roused, I have enjoyed hopping from one field to another, even if it meant missing some of the harvest. But I would not advise any young English writer to follow my example. Better to keep to one field and year after year describe the same three brown cows in it. Then people know where they are with you, cows and all. Ours is an age of specialisation. Just recently a young critic, rather an ass, announced that I was out-of-date. But I am even further out-of-date than he imagines, for in my attitude towards my work I belong to the eighteenth century, when professional authors were expected to write anything from sermons to farces. Neither Fleet Street nor Bond Street can claim me: I come from Grub Street.

My first novel, *Adam in Moonshine*, was all fine writing and nonsense, a little coloured trial balloon. But the story does not move effortlessly like a balloon: it moves stiffly, creaking with self-consciousness. Not having any press-cuttings, I do not know exactly how it was received, but I have an idea it was called 'an essayist's novel'. I do remember, however, that Arnold Bennett dismissed it with scorn, saying that it had no substance. This was true enough, but it was rather like complaining that no slice of meat could be found in a meringue. I also remember that one reader who seemed to have enjoyed it was Asquith, who told me so. It was published in America, where it was an immediate and complete failure. But during the thirty-odd years since the novel first appeared, I have met or heard from odd readers to whom it had some special appeal. 'Best thing you ever did,' they would tell me, making me feel at once that I had wasted an appalling amount of time and energy ever since bathing Adam in moonshine. What was truest in the tale was my feeling for its background, the Yorkshire Dales country, for which I had – and still have – a deep affection. It was the moors and the trout streams below them, the grey stone bridges and the whitewashed farmhouses, not the ravishing girls I tried to create, that had the magic. Only two kinds of country have made me feel homesick for them – these Dales, which after all I had known and loved since childhood, and, inexplicably, the Arizona desert, which I greeted like a lost son, as if I had once been a Pueblo Indian or a Navajo.

My second tale, *Benighted*, written late at night, was an attempt, familiar enough now but unusual then in the Twenties, to transmute the thriller into symbolical fiction with some psychological depth. I don't think I succeeded in this, though the tale itself was readable and sufficiently engrossing. There was none of this fancy work in America, where my publishers, calling it *The Old Dark House*, handled it as a thriller and sold about 20,000 copies. I refused many applications to dramatise it, believing that the queer inmates of that house would shrivel under the spotlights, but agreed to a film being made of it in Hollywood, where it became one of the early talkies and, thanks to an exceptionally good cast, was shown up and down the world for many years. The last glimpse I had of a poster advertising it was outside a cinema in the Kasbah of Algiers. If you are as prolific as I have been, you find something you have written turning up in the oddest places, travellers often obligingly reporting the discovery of a book of yours in the mysterious reaches of the Amazon or in some engineer's cabin among the icebergs. You toss a tale or some chapters of autobiography into the pool and the ripples go out and out, on and on. There are times, however, when they seem to be there and it is all a mistake. A few years ago, visiting a remote town in southern Chile, I was agreeably surprised to learn how expectant and eager the youth of the place was to greet me. They thought I was Elvis Presley.

A comparatively short tale like *Benighted* can be written, night after night, after work all day on other things. This is not possible with a long novel. And it is a mistake to imagine that a long novel – at least the kind of long novel I have written – is merely the equivalent of several average-length novels added together. It is not simply a matter of going on and on. There are of course long novels that go on and on, marching steadily from the cradle to the grave, but they have never attracted me either as a writer or a reader. My kind of long novel is really an exceptionally broad novel, the whole scene being wider than it is in a novel of ordinary length. Generally it follows the fortunes not of one central character but those of a group. A narrative of such breadth cannot be sustained without severe concentration upon it for months. It can be kept going only by a huge creative effort.

During the earlier chapters, every morning you seem to be lifting an elephant off your desk. True, if you can stick at it and avoid having a long break – I had one with a later novel and it was disastrous – you begin to gather momentum, are riding the elephant, and may find yourself in a kind of trance writing five thousand words a day, often better words than those that earlier you brought together so slowly and laboriously. Patience and industriousness may help, but what is essential to this whole enterprise is vitality, and any writer who is not sure how much energy he can release should not try a long novel. Unless he is one of the rare masters, to whom any advice of mine would be worthless, he will have to slug away and sweat it out or the whole thing will die on him. The lump must be leavened every day. This explains why, apart from the work of those masters, most long novels lack delicacy and subtlety, have a roughness of texture and coarseness of tone displeasing to fastidious persons, happy to read or even write, given time, essays on the spirit of place in Tuscany.

My share of *FarthingHall* bought me the time I needed for a long novel. I knew what kind of long novel I wanted to write. I had always been fascinated by what we, not the Spaniards, call the picaresque, ample tales in which the characters go wandering – *Don Quixote* (that supreme masterpiece), *Gil Blas*, *Tom Jones*, *Wilhelm Meister* (in parts), *Pickwick*. I saw no reason why the picaresque novel should vanish with the stage-coach. Why not one about my own England of the Twenties? No attempt to create a sort of Christmas-card past – that would have been a fake – but using as a background the England I knew and presenting it quite realistically. (Which, indeed, I did – but remember I am still referring to the background, not to the story itself.) This idea of a contemporary picaresque long novel haunted me, refusing to go when other people argued against it, even when they were people who knew, they said, what the reading public wanted and what it didn't want.

Let me add here that I didn't know, have never pretended to

know, and that in forty years of writing I doubt if I have spent
half an hour wondering what readers or audiences wanted. I
have had some bad ideas and done some rushed, scamped work
at times, but never because I was not trying to please myself
but a host of strangers. Publishers, theatre managers, editors,
agents, seem to know about public taste, but it has always been
a mystery to me. How could I aim at a target that wasn't there?
I have seen myself described, though not recently, as a shrewd
North Countryman who knew exactly how to tickle the public
fancy. This is miles out. I am not shrewd – I wish I was – and
the only fancy I know how to tickle is my own. I have always
argued that a writer, having to give so much time to his novel
or play, is a fool if he does not please himself first, before
considering readers and audiences. This explains why writers
have such a bad time in mass media, where ten clever persons
will meet every day, trying to decide how to please a lot of
stupid people they have never met.

5

This idea of a picaresque long novel aroused about as much
enthusiasm as a stuffed walrus at an exhibition of water-
colours. The long novel was out of fashion, expensive to print,
hard to sell. The picaresque was out too, except perhaps as an
excuse for fancy dress. Then my next move made matters
worse. For I decided that this story should be about a concert
party – or pierrot troupe. I knew nothing about concert parties
and had to mug them up a bit. I also visited a few towns, never
large cities, and stayed a few nights in theatrical digs. (Afterwards I had scores of letters from pros telling me I must have
spent years touring.) This decision, I was told, was fatal. The
monster I was planning would now be 'a back-stage novel',
which readers, it appeared, had always disliked.

That was not all. I had found a title that was no good. 'No, old boy; think again.' I did, once I had finished the book, so that my desk was littered with sheets on which I had scribbled possible alternatives. But it was no use, the white elephant would have to be called *The Good Companions*. Not that this title was thought to be too sentimental. That came later, when the advertisers, the calendar publishers, the photographers, with their pretty groups of puppies and kittens, saw what could be done with it. No, at that time, before the book was out, the title was thought to be too odd. This seems incredible, I know, but it is the honest truth. *The Good Companions* was no sugary commonplace when I first put the words together; all that, I repeat, came later. What also came later, so that I suffered under it for the next twenty years, was the habit, which every speaker seemed to mistake for a new and bright idea, of referring to me in public as a good companion. Many a chairman, as he turned towards me with an arch look, a coy smile, must have been astounded by the glare he got. For while among friends and in the mood I am amiable enough, even high-spirited on occasion, at no time have I made any claims to good companionship. I merely gave my novel the same name as the concert party whose adventures it described.

True, the story had a cosy fairy-tale atmosphere, which incidentally I have never tried to reproduce, although so many people, almost with tears in their eyes, have begged me to make the attempt. (Writers should never give in to such people.) The background might be contemporary and realistic, as I have already said, but what happened in front of it did suggest one of the cosier fairy tales. There are two reasons for this. The first, and less important, is that unless an author has made up his mind never to give way, a large picaresque novel lures him into this atmosphere. The second reason I understand now but was not even conscious of at the time. I had had the War, in which almost every man I had known and liked had been killed. Then, just as life was opening out, there came a period of anxiety, overwork, constant strain, ending tragically. Later, when that time was further away, I would be able to face it, not only in memory but in my work, where it can all be found in one place or another. (The Russians consider me an interesting writer but far too pessimistic for socialist realism. This is at least nearer the truth than the Jolly Jack nonsense of silly journalists here.) But first I had to find some release, give myself a holiday of the spirit while writing this novel of 250,000 words. Certainly if I had been entirely committed to novel-writing – and, as I have already suggested, I never have been – I might have taken the opposite course, dredging it all up in autobiography thinly disguised as fiction. That might have been more healing, but temperamentally I am opposed to this almost direct use of personal experiences in so-called creative work, I must find at some remove from them characters and action symbolic of my own thought and feeling. So in *The Good Companions* I gave myself a holiday from anxiety and strain and tragic circumstance, shaping and colouring a long happy daydream. And because a lot of other people then must have felt in need of such a holiday, so long a daydream, the elephant suddenly turned into a balloon.

Though the leading booksellers had been given page proofs to read, the total advance sale was only about 3,000 copies. The book cost 10s. 6d., a stiff price for a novel in 1929. Moreover, the slump had arrived. My publishers, Heinemann, having to face the expense of setting up a book of this length, risked printing 10,000 copies. If the reviews were helpful – as they proved to be – then, we thought, 7,000 or even 8,000 might be sold. I quote these figures to show what nonsense was written and talked afterwards about a shrewd author, astute publishers, booksellers who knew their customers. The book came out in July and for weeks nothing much happened. Then in autumn the balloon went up. The book had to be printed and bound all over the place, and all kinds of vans were hired to deliver it. Towards Christmas the daily sale was more than the total advance had been. This was all very exciting of course, but I was too busy to make many public appearances as a successful author: I was hard at work on another long novel, *Angel Pavement*.

The irony department was also hard at work. Jack Priestley was given a high priority up there. A modest run of luck, just beyond the limit of our expectations, would have done me much good and no possible harm. Not so this giant jackpot, this golden gusher, this genie out of the bottle. I became associated in many people's minds with all those photographs of puppies and kittens that soon appeared. The vast public I reached was disappointed and then suspicious when I did not come along with more and more good companions: what was the matter with this chap? In literary circles, where my earlier books had usually had a friendly reception, I was now seen as a sort of Quisling of letters. No longer a man and a brother, I was something called 'a best-seller'. I could now be condemned without being read. Clever youngsters, growing up, would have nothing to do with a writer who had pleased silly Aunt Kate, stupid old Uncle James. A whole generation of the more literate and intellectual types, the young who pick and choose sharply among older writers, swept by me, its nose in the air. If I had written *Anna Karenina* now, it would have been assumed, among the élite, that I was still turning out twaddle for the mob.

Some people have said that I was the victim of jealousy and envy. I do not agree with them. It was not my fellow novelists, competing for the public's attention, who would allow me no literary reputation. What I suffered from was the fixed idea, itself an indictment of our whole culture, that anything widely popular must necessarily be bad. Criticism, the worst not the best, borrowed 'best-seller' from the book trade, where it means what it says and nothing more, and made it pejorative. I thought this bad criticism then; I still think it is. A writer's sales are the concern of publishers, agents and booksellers; the critic should mind his own business, concentrating on the writer's work. If this work seems to the critic to have been cynically debased in an effort to reach popularity, then he is entitled to say so. But clearly the work must be read and considered first. Sales-figures criticism is simply a fraud.

Now the novels I have written are full of faults, some of which I hope to indicate. But that they are faulty because I tried to keep the popularity I had won, so unexpectedly as I have shown, with *The Good Companions*, I do most sharply deny. Had that been my aim I would have kept on writing the same kind of novel, one fairy tale after another in contemporary settings, whereas in fact I resisted every appeal to do so. Whatever *Angel Pavement* may or may not be, it is certainly not another *Good Companions*. Of course a writer cannot escape his own temperament. If I am extroverted, I cannot pretend to be introverted, just because introversion is in fashion. If instinctively, when writing a novel, I show men in their relation to the outer world, then the fiction of their inner world is not for me. I can well believe that very fastidious readers could not enjoy my novels, finding them too hearty, too coarse in grain, too broadly humorous. But then I am not a very fastidious person myself. If there is an élite, I don't belong to it. If there is a streak of vulgarity in my work, that is because there is a streak of vulgarity in me. I am not delicate and subtle in my tastes; I prefer artists in the major tradition to minor masters; it does not worry me to have to share my favourites with so many other people; I have enjoyed books, music, pictures, but without despising music-halls and football matches. Now that I am elderly, gouty, a bit cantankerous, I dislike crowds whatever they may be doing, but for a long time I did not avoid them but sought them out, and if they were happy then I was happy too.

After the First War, when the embittered introverts took over, affection was banished from literature. The most admired writers had none of it. The critics who did the admiring were without it. The readers who admired the critics hadn't much of it. Affection was out. It was as if literature now belonged to querulous and egocentric invalids. Anybody more robust merely provided or enjoyed entertainment. But fiction and drama, impure art forms that must not be confused with painting or music, begin as entertainment. *Don Quixote* and *Hamlet* are entertainments that have lasted a long time and, broadening and deepening with the centuries, have turned into great literature. As I have never completely identified myself with the novel, I am not thinking about myself when I say I have always disliked the sneering reference to 'popular novelists', apparently not worth naming, by lecturers in Eng. Lit. departments. After all it is much easier to get by in Eng. Lit. than it is to become and then remain a popular novelist. A much smaller amount of energy, imagination and courage is required. Most of the popular novelists I have known have been far more vital human beings than the average Eng. Lit. type.

Thinking about my novels, which, to be honest, is something I have never done before, I can discover various reasons why I failed to establish myself solidly as a novelist, as perhaps I ought to have done. But not one of them, I must repeat, has anything to do with maintaining or regaining popularity. I never made any attempt to return to where I had once succeeded, never tried for another *Good Companions*, another *Angel Pavement*, which, after all, sold several hundred thousand copies. The truth is, I never really identified myself with the novel. I never saw myself as a man who was either a novelist or nothing. And indeed from 1932 onwards I wrote far more plays than novels. Even when I turned from the Theatre to books, it was not always to write fiction.

What was behind all this hopping from novels to plays to autobiographical-descriptive books? Possibly a fundamental lack of what I appeared superficially to have in abundance – self-confidence. Perhaps I was afraid of committing myself to any one thing. Perhaps I hopped about so that I made a difficult target. But I was not conscious of this at the time. I had a great deal of energy, many ideas for work of different kinds, and could never resist a technical challenge, problems of technique having a fascination for me. Some of these problems I think I solved skilfully; but if anybody declares that serious artists do not amuse themselves in this fashion, I have no reply. When I was in my middle teens, certain that I would never be a wool merchant but not sure if I would be a writer, an actor, or a musician, my father sensibly warned me more than once that I might turn out to be a Jack of all trades, master of none. Even as early as 1924, when he died, he would have admitted that he had been wrong. But sometimes now I think he may have been right.

Some of the novels disappointed me, as well as a great many other people, because the ideas with which I began failed to sustain me throughout fairly long narratives. Perhaps I made too early a start, not giving them time to act properly as catalysts of creation. So these novels were not what I had intended them to be. They may have had good scenes and passages in them, but their total effect was unsatisfactory. They didn't come off. This is true of *Faraway*, planned as a symbolic tale of a treasure hunt, though this novel suffered too from a long break in the writing, during the time when I visited the South Seas, where some of the action took place. In Tahiti I had long talks with James Norman Hall, who greatly admired *Angel Pavement* but had to write to me, after *Faraway* came out, to tell me how disappointing he found it. Hall, like his friend and collaborator, Charles Nordhoff, was an American who had settled in Tahiti, marrying a Tahitian girl. It was they who revived the *Bounty* story that seems to fascinate Hollywood. Hall was a modest, unambitious writer but unusually impressive as a man, quiet, with a twinkling charm, and absolutely honest. He was quite right to be disappointed. I didn't blame him; I was disappointed too.

It is also true, and now with no extenuating circumstances, of a later novel called *They Walk in the City*. Here I began with the idea of two provincial young lovers who kept losing and finding each other in London, to them a vast stone forest. Incidentally, I wrote much of it in Arizona, just as I described the desert there not on the spot but five or six thousand miles away, in Highgate Village. Except when he is actually reporting, a writer should remove himself as far as possible from the scene he is trying to describe, for what the memory retains is all the reader needs to know. But I made a hash of this novel, *They Walk in the City*. It ends in melodrama, and not even good melodrama. I had to finish the thing somehow, wanting to get rid of it, not because I thought it worthless – there are some good things in it – but because I knew I had failed to realise my idea. If I had such a novel on my hands now, when I lead a quiet life, I would put it on one side, hoping to return to it and make it better; but at that time, in the middle Thirties, I was a kind of three-ring circus of authorship. I had undertaken to do so much that almost everything I did was hit-or-miss. Though I had planned to write a big ambitious novel, in which there was to be far more social criticism than the babes-in-the-woods theme might suggest, *They Walk in the City* was a miss, not because reviewers and readers didn't like it (I can't remember now how it was received) but because I didn't. And I have never spent five minutes with it since I passed the proofs, if I did pass the proofs. Serves me right.

There were other novels, now deservedly neglected, that bounced into the fiction lists, found plenty of readers there, and perhaps made their effect before they were forgotten. They were deliberately polemical, journalistic, social-moral fables. One was *Wonder Hero*, in which I brought together the expensive antics of the mass dailies, fighting a circulation war in those early Thirties, and the bleak despair I had found in the depressed areas. Another was *Three Men in New Suits*, which I wrote quickly when the last war was ending. Nobody need tell me that novels of this sort do not make lasting contributions to the art of fiction. I knew that when I wrote them. I think now I might have done more good by writing directly on these various subjects – for example, *English Journey* is more effective than *Wonder Hero* where they have any common ground – but I didn't think so then. I believed that a great many people would read something that called itself a novel when they would never dream of looking at any piece of social criticism. (This is not true now, but I think it was in the Thirties and Forties.) The danger of this hasty topical novel-writing is that while taking so wide an aim you may hit nothing except your own reputation, failing to give your readers a story that satisfies them and equally failing to convert them to your point of view. I was not unaware of this danger at the time, but, tempted, I fell, and more than once.

A novel of a different kind, very much a product of war time but one that I think does not deserve to be forgotten, is *Daylight on Saturday*. As nobody ever mentions it, I must explain that it is a novel about an aircraft factory during the war, and it is something of a technical achievement because it never moves outside the factory. It was far from being a hastily improvised novel. I was allowed to visit a number of aircraft factories and talked to all kinds of people engaged in the industry. The ground, whatever I may have finally pulled out of it, was thoroughly prepared. And the novel itself was planned with considerable care. These people worked such long hours that in winter it was only on Saturday that they saw daylight – hence my title – and after watching them and listening to them I felt I ought to take as much trouble with my work as they had to do with theirs. On the jacket of the only copy I seem to possess, Edwin Muir, not an easy man to please, is quoted as saying, in a *Listener* review, that this was by far my best novel. (It was published in 1943.) Whatever its value as fiction, I hope it will not be altogether forgotten, for I should like to think that some English readers, during the next fifty years, might learn from it how people lived and worked in World War Two. Moreover, confined to its factory, *Daylight on Saturday* does attempt to explore the relations between men and women who have to work together, and all too few English novels have tried to do this.

Here, as elsewhere, I was not following anybody's example. Because, on the one hand, I was a novelist of talent not of genius, and because, on the other hand, I was never wildly eccentric in manner, I think such originality as I had was hardly ever acknowledged. But I really was my own man in fiction. I was not doing all over again what older novelists had done. I may have been as extroverted as Wells and Bennett were, for instance, and may have shared their sociological interests; I could not pretend to be an entirely different kind of man; but the way in which I dealt with my characters and related them to their social backgrounds was in fact quite individual. When I published my first two long novels, there were references to Dickens. These were silly. Having had to write about him, I know a great deal more about Dickens now than I did when I was writing those long novels, when in fact I had not even read Dickens for years. (Fielding was the only possible influence among the old novelists, and outside fiction the only direct influence came from Hazlitt, whom I read with passion in my early twenties.) I realise that talent may be unconsciously imitative, as genius never is, but looking back on my novels and trying to be honest about them, I still see the more important of them as individual experiments, nothing revolutionary, nothing for the textbooks, but, even so, genuine experiments. I was never trying to write like somebody else. That would have been boring, and I was always determined not to bore myself, no matter what happened to readers.

Novels of talent, unlike those of genius, may be mistimed, coming out too soon or too late. This happened to the longest novel I ever wrote – 275,000 words, making ferocious demands on a writer in his later fifties – that I called *Festival at Farbridge*. I wanted to write a large-scale comic novel about postwar England – some of the younger novelists had the comic vision, but it was far too restricted – and, stupidly as I see now, I chose the 1951 Festival of Britain, which I welcomed and never sneered at, as a peg on which to hang the tale. Its reception disappointed me as that of no other novel of mine has done. Even now, ten years later, I can still feel the sting, if only because I know, as nobody else can, how long and hard I worked at this novel. The popular dailies, chiefly for political reasons, were hostile to the Festival itself. (Since then some overseas visitors have told me that 1951 was the last time they saw Britain splendidly alive.) The intellectual reviewers were sour about the novel, possibly because they disliked my kind of high spirits, possibly too because they felt I was baiting them and their kind, overlooking the fact that I dealt with very different types in exactly the same spirit. So this big gun misfired. What can I say? I realise that humour not on the highest possible level changes with each generation, coming into and going out of fashion like hats and waistcoats, so all I can do now is to assure those readers and playgoers who have ever been amused by anything I have written that here, in *Festival at Farbridge*, are some of the funniest scenes I have ever imagined, and that this is not simply my own opinion. And to this day, so far as I know, it remains the only attempt at a comic wide panorama of post-war England. One of its admirers was Cyril Joad, who had his affectations but also had a good mind, and I like to remember that he found himself entertained by it at a time when, already in the grip of the cancer that killed him, he needed all the entertainment he could find.

I am not one for favourites, and I have always been irritated by questions about my favourite this, that and the other. But if I have a favourite among my novels, it is *Bright Day*, which I wrote towards the end of the war. If I were to be judged on evidence supplied by one single novel, my own choice would not be *Angel Pavement*, in spite of the solid support it has had, but *Bright Day*. There are several good reasons for this. One of them is that in this novel I did not fail the idea with which I began, in spite of considerable technical difficulties, the constant shift of time, atmosphere, tone. Another is that although the story is not at all autobiographical – the first-person narrator, Gregory Dawson, is a writer, it is true, but both his work and his attitude towards it are quite different from mine – I was able to recreate, in the scenes recollected from Dawson's youth, something of the life I had known before 1914, and not, I believe, without colour, warmth and tenderness. And it does seem to me even now, though of course I may still be flattering myself, that I did succeed in weaving into one fabric many different fibres: Dawson's personal history and that of the Alington family, the changing social scene, the ironies that passing time leaves behind. It may be all a little naïve for our most brilliant contemporary minds; but then so am I. And here for once, try as I might, I cannot grumble, for *Bright Day* was generally received as I hoped it would be, and among the many people who read the book were some I was delighted to please. One of them was Jung, who wrote me a long letter about it.

If that remark about readers seems arrogant, it is being misinterpreted. The readers I was delighted to please were those I knew, a microscopic fraction. And not only do I not know all the other readers, I cannot even imagine them. Millions and millions of my novels have been sold, in many different languages all over the world, yet I have never been able to imagine who read them, and often, setting aside friends and acquaintances, I have felt that nobody was reading them. And this is easier to feel nowadays than it was when I first began writing novels, because more people send appreciative letters to young authors than they do to elderly authors, and anyhow letter-writing itself is dying out. I have a theory, probably shared by many colleagues, that the readers who have kept alongside me down the years, not always pleased but ready to try again with every new novel, are nice shy people, the very last in any room who would come up and tell me what they had liked.

Other writers will know what I mean when I say that of the thousands of remarks that have been made to me about my work nineteen out of every twenty have been idiotic. In all the English-speaking countries there still exists a social practice designed to put a scribbler almost at ease in decent society. Shortly after he has been introduced, a writer is tossed some perfunctory and faintly patronising remark about something he once wrote. It is a practice that should be discontinued.

Dear sir or madam, we are all flattered by any intelligent discussion of what we have done, without too much sugar and cream too, but, if you don't know and don't care, then leave our books out of the conversation. Men have grabbed hold of me, often yanking me away from talk I wanted to hear, to tell me that once, years ago, they read a novel of mine, giving me the impression they had pulled me out of a burning building.

One curious by-product of fiction, for those who write it, is worth mentioning. To imagine intensely is to add to experience. We remember scenes we wrote long after we have forgotten our daily life at that time. Sometimes we have to remind ourselves that we were not there, except in imagination. When we begin a novel, which is what most of us do only when we have run out of excuses for not beginning it, we are hesitant and have no confidence in ourselves, probably writing the opening paragraph over and over again. We are like small children who creep up to the sea, put a toe in, then scamper to safety. But once we are writing steadily we return in the morning to the dark road, the brilliant crowded room, the ship among the flying fish, whatever scene we left the night before, and in five minutes the sustained fable seems to be life, while all the life surrounding us is as thin and flickering as a dream. Then, years afterwards, as we wander among our memories, we are standing on that dark road again, we are looking down on that brilliant crowded room, leaning over the rail of the upper deck we watch the flying fish once more. Our experience has been enlarged and enriched by the inventions of our trade. Nobody looking at us could guess all that we have seen and known. We have lived more lives than one.

Before leaving books for plays, the decent calm of publishers' offices for the gaudy merry-go-round of the Theatre, I cannot ignore the only serious plan I failed to carry through. It was for a trilogy, not of novels but of what I called, setting a small fashion, 'chapters of autobiography'. They used the device, convenient if sometimes wearisome, of packing reminiscence and discourse into a long reverie, begun and ended at a certain time in a definite place. I published two out of the three as *Midnight on the Desert* and *Rain upon Godshill*. I had planned to write the third volume in or near one of those groves of giant sequoias in California which are like arboreal cathedrals. But the war came, and many years went by before I saw California again. I have sometimes thought of completing the trilogy by cramming twenty years into one volume, and calling it *Instead of the Trees*, but it would be too widely removed from the other two both in form and spirit. The man who wrote it would be another man, living in another world. So my original design, finally to reprint all three in one volume, was never fulfilled, and to this day both *Midnight on the Desert* and *Rain upon Godshill*, like parts of an unfinished building, seem to me to exist in an air of melancholy and neglect. I try to forget them.

6

It was in May 1932 that I arrived in the London Theatre. The play was *Dangerous Corner*. It was brilliantly directed by Tyrone Guthrie, who introduced many new devices that are now commonplaces of production, and, though it had no star part, Flora Robson's performance dominated it. The irony department had me followed through the stage door. The play itself was a trick thing, in which time divided at the sound of a musical cigarette-box. I wrote it in a week, chiefly to prove that a man might produce long novels and yet be able to write effectively, using the strictest economy, for the stage. It was so poorly received by the daily press – 'This is Mr Priestley's first play and we don't mind if it is also his last': that kind of welcome – that there was talk on the Saturday of taking it off, after five performances. If it had been taken off that night, I doubt if the play would ever have been heard of again. But with more favourable Sunday notices, especially from James Agate and Ivor Brown, it had a comfortable run, and six years later it was revived.

The irony department's contribution can now be assessed. Here was a play I wrote very quickly, as a technical experiment and as proof that I could write for the stage. (Not that I knew everything. I didn't know – or had forgotten – that West End audiences, no matter how tense the scene, have to laugh every few minutes, and that if you don't provide them with something they will laugh at anything.) It was received in Shaftesbury Avenue so tepidly that only my own insistence carried it past five performances. It then became the most popular play I have ever written. I doubt if there is any country in the world possessing a playhouse that has not seen *Dangerous Corner*, or if any other play written during the last thirty years has had more performances. Oddly enough, exactly the same pattern was repeated, after the war, when the Old Vic produced a new play of mine, *An Inspector Calls*. Again, it had a cool, almost hostile, reception. Again, it went all over the world, having 1,600 performances (for which I received a total fee of ten pounds from the Foreign Office) in Germany alone. Possibly the same thing could happen all over again next season, if I could prove I had not lost all skill and had sufficient patience to try once more. It is not the writing that demands patience – a book like *Literature and Western Man* is a greater test of endurance than half-a-dozen plays – but what happens after the writing is done. It is as if an author of books had to find not only the right publisher but also the right paper-maker, the right compositors and machinists, the right binders, the right salesmen.

All British and American playwrights – I cannot speak for those elsewhere – will agree with me when I say that the success or failure of theatrical production is largely determined by chance and accident. Theatre people tend to be superstitious, and I don't blame them. Once through the stage door, you might as well believe in astrology. Some plays attract good fortune, others bad. Nothing can be done about it. By the time you realise – and this may be weeks before the London opening – that a production is heavy with doom, you are helplessly committed, surrounded by people who have contracts, and can only brace yourself to meet the next disaster. On the other hand, if the gods have decided in your favour, then everything comes right: the actors you want are free; the London theatre best suited to your play is available; you open at exactly the right time. You cannot justly claim any credit for this, just as you cannot justly be blamed for the disasters. Yet in the circumstances of production in the English-speaking Theatre you are compelled to exist in an over-heated atmosphere of dazzling successes and shameful flops, you are a wonder man in October, a pretentious clown in March, you are in, you are out. Hardly anybody can be found in theatrical London or New York who takes you for what you really are – neither a genius nor a fraud but simply a man trying to do a difficult job as best he can, a writer who does not deserve to make a fortune out of one lucky hit and equally does not deserve to have his work unrewarded and derided. No competent English or American playwright is as good or as bad as managers, theatrical press and public say he is: they are playing roulette with him.

It is this gaming-house atmosphere that makes serious work in the Theatre so difficult in the English-speaking countries. You feel you have one foot in the playhouse and the other in the Stock Exchange. If racehorses could think and talk, they could

usefully hold joint sessions with the British and American
leagues of dramatists. There is far too much of the wrong kind
of excitement. Everything seems to be happening at three in
the morning. One year, after a hit, an English playwright will
have half the producers in New York on the telephone to him:
the next year the same men will behave as if they had never
even heard of him. Not having any real standards of their own
or any confidence in their own judgment, theatre people in
New York and London wonder wildly who might at the
moment be in possession of the magic lamp or ring. All this has
nothing to do with dramatic art; it is not even sensible
business; it is an attempt to live in the *Arabian Nights*. Money
is squandered, time and tempers are lost, not following a
policy but hastily improvising productions that are so many
backed hunches, poker hands waiting for the other ace.

It was my suspicion and dislike of this atmosphere that kept
me away from the Theatre until I knew my children's food and
clothing could be paid for, and it was out of a desire to escape
the worst effects, once I was working in the Theatre, that I
formed my own production company. This took me into the
thick of it, but for some years I enjoyed being there, working
on the production side with friends like Irene Hentschel and
Basil Dean and Michael MacOwan, and on the managerial
side with other friends like A. D. Peters, J. P. Mitchelhill and
Thane Parker. Working in the Theatre with people is tricky,
especially if you are the author as well, because in there, away
from daylight and common sense, everybody knows best. Not
being really sure of anything, we all pretend to be absolutely
certain about everything. So friendship, as distinct from the
false good-fellowship that comes and goes so quickly, prevents
colleagues from turning into so many irritants. To work in the
Theatre with people you dislike is a torment. Where is the
Great Theatre, to which a man might be attached for years,

surrounded by friends? It is for an Englishman on the far side
of the fields of paradise.

Shaw did not approve of my production company. (I must
add here that with one enterprise or another I did help some
other dramatists to reach the public.) At that time Shaw was
declaring that any manager who revived his plays at cheap
prices would make a fortune. He had only to make a telephone
call or two and then find his cheque-book to begin testing the
truth of this assertion, but he never did. He told me – more
than once, I think – that management would ruin me: it was a
short cut to bankruptcy. He was quite wrong.

This was in the Thirties, when we could produce *Laburnum
Grove* or *Eden End* or *Time and the Conways* for about £800,
and the weekly running costs – the 'get-out' or 'nut' – were
round about the same figure, theatre and all. The profits, of
course, were never gigantic. Today's dashing characters,
operating through a network of companies, would probably
need a reading glass to see our figures. But then I was never a
showman. I don't like showmen, who always promise more
than they can perform. I dislike the whole 'show biz' side of the
Theatre, all the razzle-dazzle, glitter and glamour. Music-
halls I loved – and I owe some of my early education to Moss
and Stoll – but I prefer the legitimate stage to be quiet, solid,
bourgeois. That Great Theatre I mentioned would not be a
showman-impresario's, not a director's nor an actor's, but an
authors' theatre. If this seems strange, I must point out that
dramatic history has nearly always been made by authors'
theatres. I think I explained why this should be so, from
Shakespeare, Calderon and Molière to Chekhov and Synge, in
a little book, based on a lecture, called *The Art of the Dramatist*.

In the English-speaking Theatre I was always a divided
man, one part of me genuinely devoted to writing for the stage
and to all the tasks of production, the other part disliking the

climate and atmosphere in which productions had to live. The truth is, strange though it may seem, playgoers in Britain and America, Australia and Canada are still defying, unconsciously by this time, the prohibitions of the puritans. People do not approach the playhouse as they would a concert hall or an exhibition of pictures. They cannot take playgoing easily and naturally. They arrange theatre parties, to have a night out. They book seats at a ticket agency as they would order champagne for a spree. The whole thing is gay and rather giddy. And the popular dailies, wonderfully perceptive of their readers' weaknesses, encourage this attitude of mind. Actors and actresses are not seen as hard-working serious performers, which most of them are, but as glamorous figures, sexual images, success symbols. The best of them very creditably try to escape from this thick atmosphere of silliness, but it can easily corrupt the weaker-minded, soon turning eager conscientious youngsters into vain public darlings always breaking their promises. It is not acting itself, as some people seem to think, that corrupts them: it is this peculiar atmosphere in which our Theatre exists.

If I was often thought, as I believe I was, to be difficult and surly in the Theatre, it was chiefly because I held out, perhaps too stiffly, against this giddiness and silliness. I never led a fashionable playwright's life, attending all first nights, rushing from dressing-room to dressing-room, sitting up till two listening to theatre gossip. I worked but never played much in the hothouse. I am not now deriding the way in which good actors and actresses concentrate on their play to the exclusion of all other interests. Indeed, I have always admired this single-minded devotion. I remember a rehearsal in the middle of the war, when Irene Hentschel was producing a piece of mine called *They Came to a City*, in which I dramatised various attitudes towards the post-war world, a bit roughly perhaps, though it pleased and excited a lot of people both in London and the provinces. Three members of the cast were in their seventies. There had been an air-raid the previous night. If they had been late, these three old players, or had stayed away, trying to catch up with the sleep they had lost, nobody could have blamed them. But there they were, all three, walking up planks, standing on orange boxes, happily and devotedly rehearsing; and as I watched I marvelled. But then such players deserve a better Theatre than we have given them.

It is this peculiar atmosphere of giddiness and silliness that seems to have robbed the English-speaking Theatre of any sensible continuing tradition. It produces Shakespeare or something written last month. A repertory of substantial plays does not exist in this country. No matter how hard, and, on the whole, successfully he works, a dramatist here cannot establish with managements and leading players the kind of relation an author has with his publishers. As an agent once said to me: 'You are only as good as your last play.' But this of course is monstrous. It suggests that dramatists, with personalities and techniques of their own, are not recognised as such by this Theatre, which asks only for suppliers of plays, so much stage fodder. If novelists and essayists had been treated in this fashion, we should have hardly anything to read.

It means too that, if you miss the target, you are given no second try. And you may miss the target for a variety of reasons. A play may come on at the wrong time, when play-goers are not ready for it. Just after the war I wrote two plays one after the other. One was concerned with an elderly professor and his wife (they were played superbly by Lewis Casson and Sybil Thorndike) and their family in post-war provincial England, accepting or rebelling against the austerities of the time. *The Linden Tree* ran for 422 per-formances, and during the earlier months it could have filled two theatres. The second play, *Home is Tomorrow,* was about a United Nations special agency on a tropical island. Leslie Banks and Irene Worth headed an unusually good cast, and one or two scenes in this production brought me as much satisfaction as any work of mine on the stage. (Altogether, I think, twenty-seven plays: there is a twenty-eighth, being produced on the Continent, that I have never seen performed.) But this second play lasted only a few weeks. I may be deceiving myself – we easily do – when I say that it is as sound and strong a piece of dramatic writing as the successful *Linden Tree.* What I am certain about is that most of the dramatic critics, most of the people who attend first nights or book stalls as soon as they can, neither knew nor cared anything about the United Nations and its special agencies: I would have done better with an audience of Eskimos. If the play had any merit – as I believe, though I will admit that its action was complicated and demanded an alert audience – then its production was mistimed. Ten years later, in 1958, what left so many critics and playgoers bewildered before might have been easily understood. (Curiously enough, as I write this, the main action of the play is quite topical.) Some readers may want to tell me that they have seen this play on television. They saw something, a good try in another medium, but my *Home is Tomorrow* vanished in the November fogs of 1948.

I know how much money has been wasted trying to 'nurse' plays that opened badly. But there are some plays, solid and a bit difficult, perhaps compelled to open in an unsuitable theatre, that really can be 'nursed', and I believe that *Home is Tomorrow* was one of them. But even by 1948 the economics were too steep. If it had cost as much in 1932 to keep *Dangerous Corner* running past itself, that play would have also vanished, never to be heard of again. Modest costs of production and low 'get-outs' befriend the writer. He will never feel comfortable and at home in the showman's hit-or-miss big money Theatre. He will be allowed fewer and fewer experiments. His life in the Theatre will hang on a few press notices.

I was generally supposed to be embroiled in a permanent feud with dramatic critics. (Bob Benchley, writing in the *New Yorker* about some play of mine he didn't enjoy, ended his notice: 'Now shoot me, Mr Priestley!') Apart from the fact that I often look and sound like a man ready to quarrel with anybody, I cannot understand why I was thought to dislike the critics so much. I did less wrangling with them in public than many other playwrights. Several of them, notably Ivor Brown, were friends of mine. Agate welcomed me most warmly into the Theatre. I received much kindness and many handsome compliments from dramatic critics. The consistently unfriendly notices appeared in papers that, for one reason or another, disliked me anyhow. One influential critic, dead now, did contrive to annoy me every time I produced a new play. If it was a serious play, he would say it was all very well but disappointing because it lacked 'that rich North Country humour we expect from Mr Priestley'. If it was a comedy, he would say it was amusing enough but disappointing again because it lacked 'the serious treatment of a serious theme we expect from Mr Priestley'. For him and his readers apparently I was always writing the wrong play. And I must admit that whenever I made any experiment I immediately lost all the older critics, who declared at once that it was pretentious and that they remembered something just like it in Berlin in 1923. Time after time I was condemned for writing plays that either had too much social content or were too experimental. Not long ago I heard the most successful of our young manager-directors, on television, declaring that old British dramatists could be ignored because their work had not sufficient social content and was never experimental. Ah well!

The most considerable experiments I made are not to be found in the so-called 'Time plays', though these did reflect my interest, during those years, in the whole problem of Time. I knew Dunne, the theorist of Serialism, and when *Time and the Conways* was running he asked me if he could come and give a talk to the cast. With that innocence which seems to belong to mathematicians and engineers, and Dunne had been both, he covered a blackboard with mathematical formulae and threw over his shoulder various references to Minkowski and the Michelson-Morley experiment with the speed of light. Pretending to know what he was talking about, the players gave a magnificent performance. No, it was not in the 'Time plays' but in *Johnson Over Jordan* and *Music at Night*, which came later, that I took such dramatic technique as I possessed as far as it would go, using the most objective form there is for material that was entirely and deeply subjective, trying to take my characters outside ordinary passing time altogether and to create, you might say, a four-dimensional drama. I am not announcing that I succeeded, but I did have a thundering good try, and, if anybody is trying harder now, good luck to him or her. The new dramatists have at least one advantage, for now their critics never were in Berlin in 1923.

Once I had to do some acting of a sort in the West End, for about ten performances. This was not a publicity stunt but an attempt to save a farcical comedy, *When We Are Married*, that had just opened and finally had a long run. Frank Pettingell, who played the comic lead, a drunken West Riding photographer, was injured in a motor accident, so Basil Dean, a man not easily denied, rushed me on as a drunken West Riding photographer, at least a part not obviously beyond my physical and mental range, no Hamlet or Romeo. I cannot say if I was a good or bad actor, but I certainly knew my own lines, never fluffed or 'dried', and duly got my laughs. I didn't enjoy the experience. I seemed to be always waiting for a climax, a moment of truth and glory, that never arrived. Probably because I was not really an actor, I found it all curiously elusive, frustrating, unrewarding. And to paint one's face after an early lunch, all for the benefit of matinée audiences, waiting for the tea they had ordered, was horrible. Perhaps it was then that I began to dislike audiences, enjoying rehearsals of my plays but avoiding performances of them. In London especially, people giggle and guffaw too easily: they visit a theatre to be tickled. I always preferred if possible to open plays in the North, where they sat with tightened lips and narrowed eyes, grimly awaiting their money's worth.

Because I have suggested that some players are soon corrupted by the atmosphere in which our Theatre exists, this does not mean I dislike actors and actresses in general. On the contrary, I remember them with gratitude and affection. Whenever I tried to escape from routine playmaking, it was among them, rather than among managers, critics and public, that I found enthusiastic allies. I don't know what conditions are like now, but in the Thirties particularly they were very hard for minor players. Auditions or a series of interviews with men and women desperate for work could be almost heartbreaking. I remember a woman, now a fairly well-known character actress, who began rehearsing badly, not only because she was very nervous but also because, as we discovered later, she was half-fainting from starvation. All this was detestable. Discipline, necessary in the Theatre, should be artistic not economic. And what made auditions and interviews at once so embarrassing and touching was the determination of the players, those who realised they had no hope of getting a part, to carry it off in a gallant debonair manner, as if they were paying us a social call rather than seeking a livelihood. It is this brave bearing of the actor, hoping against hope, that makes one's heart go out to him. He seemed at such times the symbolic figure of our species, creatures who dream like demigods but know they must soon die and be forgotten. When a play of mine failed, it was not wounded vanity but feeling for the actors, smiling to the end, that hurt me most. Once I was compelled against my will to go away, to leave a sinking production. I cannot think of it even now without feeling a rat.

I look back on a fine procession of leading ladies: Angela Baddeley, Edna Best, Jean Forbes-Robertson, Ursula Jeans, Beatrix Lehmann, Margaret Leighton, Flora Robson, Frances Rowe, Lydia Sherwood, Jessica Tandy, Sybil Thorndike, Estelle Winwood, Googie Withers, Irene Worth, to name no more, curtsy and smile as the curtain of memory rises. I hope I shan't offend these ladies – nor Wilfrid Lawson, whose eruptive yet wonderfully controlled performance in *I Have Been Here Before* I can never forget – if I say that the player who comes soonest to mind is Ralph Richardson. We worked together in five plays, two of which I wrote for him. He has said in print that mine were the speeches that pleased him most, and I am not returning cutlet for cutlet when I say as much about his acting. Just as I am not the 'plain down-to-earth writer' that many people have called me, Richardson is not, as I have so often seen him described, the ordinary Englishman enlarged. And not simply because of his unusual range and flexibility of tone. (His was the only Falstaff of our time.) Mixed with his large helping of ordinary elements is one that never came out of the earth. He is a kind of Bully Bottom providing his own enchanted glade. For a while he may seem as commonplace as some familiar town, but then suddenly, above that town, a strange moon is rising. He can be a bank clerk, an insurance agent, a dentist, but very soon mysterious lights and shadows, tones of anguish and ecstasy, are discovered in banking, insurance and dentistry. He should always have big challenging parts; with anything smaller he deliberately deploys so much technique that he fantasticates it, perhaps to amuse himself, like a master violinist asked to play some drawing-room piece. In *Johnson Over Jordan* I handed him, as they say, a packet. It made outrageous demands on his skill and endurance without bringing him all the rewards he deserved. That we remained friends, as indeed we are still, is partly explained by the fact that we have common interests outside the Theatre, for he is not all actor, just as I am not all author. And each of us thinks the other a fine fellow – but a bit cracked.

Twice, and only twice, has a play of mine so wrung me I could no longer see. The first occasion was in 1938, at the final performance of *Johnson Over Jordan*. The end of this play, when Johnson said his farewell and then turned to go towards the glitter of stars, the blue-dark spaces, the unknown (and how Basil Dean contrived to suggest such cosmic depth, I have never understood) while Britten's *finale* sounded from the orchestra pit, moved most people any and every night. But this was the last night, the last farewell, the last glimpse of Johnson against that starry sky, the last sound of Britten's triumphant crescendo – never, never again – and I might have been staring into a grave. The second occasion was in 1946. I was visiting Vienna, still darkened, torn, divided by the war. At the delicious old Josefstädter Theater they were doing *Time and the Conways*. A translation had been hidden for years from the Nazis, who had banned all my work. Now the Viennese could produce it, which they did exquisitely. But there was something else. Here I must explain that the middle act of this play jumps forward twenty years, showing us what has happened to the young hopefuls of Act One, to whom we return, still having their party, in Act Three. In London and

New York we had on the whole compromised in the ages of our casts, not too old for the first and third acts, not too young for the second. But the director of the Josefstädter had used really young players. This meant that Act Two was rather too wiggy and a little uncertain. But when youth, so confident in the future, so eager to experience it, so *young*, returned in Act Three, the play was stronger, more poignant, than ever before. And to this must be added the whole circumstances of the production, the enchanting old playhouse, Vienna itself dark and ravaged; and then again, for me, flashing memories of where and how I had written this scene or that, years before in another time and place, almost another world. The total effect was overwhelming. Perhaps it is more sensible to write books and not plays, but it is not out of books such moments arrive, beautiful and terrible.

How were these plays written? Well, different men, different methods. I remember Shaw telling me how he would regard a play he was doing as a sort of spoken opera – a duet would be followed by a trio, a trio by a quartette, then an ensemble, and so on. Barrie told me how he would plan a play, and then would often write what seemed the weakest act first, to make sure that would work before wasting time on the other two acts. I tried this method once, writing a third act first, but then found it had all to be rewritten. The irony of my play-writing was that the comedies, which it was generally supposed I had tossed off between serious efforts, actually took most time and gave me most trouble. The actual writing of the serious plays never took long. Driving myself hard, I often wrote them in about ten days. But of course I had given them a lot of thought beforehand. When an idea struck me, I would scribble a few words in a little black notebook – I have it still, its pages filled with ideas for plays that will never be written now – and of course it was those ideas that set the imagination working that finally became plays. The few serious ideas that gave me most trouble – I did four careful versions of one – never even saw the stage. The plays I wrote at top speed could be rehearsed successfully with hardly any changes, though I never had a play printed before production, always regarding the prompt copy as the final text. I may be told that I ought to have taken more time, to give every speech a richer flavour. But though I constantly experimented with dramatic form, I was still working within the tradition of English realism. Too much enrichment of speech would have destroyed this realism. An English audience would have begun to ask who I thought these people were. Not being Irish or American, I had at least to lull all suspicion by starting with a familiar thin, flat idiom, before I began cheating. An English dramatist has the hardest task of all. He has to make scenes out of people who don't want to make a scene.

It is hard to avoid melancholy cadences in any account of work in the Theatre. We remember not only the failures that might have been avoided but also the successes already fading in older people's memories. The plays themselves may be in print, but they were written to be seen and heard, not read. And in a Theatre like ours, which asks for something either new or very old, such plays have vanished. A few ageing players, as they wipe the grease-paint and cold cream off their faces, recollect the plays' triumphant first appearances. It is all going, going, gone: a lift of the voice, a gesture, a look, that were marvels and things of beauty in their time. So, thinking about the Theatre, I cling to my belief that in its own time, somewhere along the fourth dimension, everything still exists: that lift of the voice, that gesture, that look, they are still there. Sometimes I wonder how many people, apart from technologists and journalists, are genuinely excited by all the talk about travel in space, by this desire to leave the earth for nothingness. I know that, when I think about the Theatre, I only wonder when at least some part of our minds will be able to travel in time, to recapture the past that has not really vanished at all, to see the old velvet curtains rising and falling again, to applaud once more the brave players.

7

Film needs no time-travelling. Here on the screen – looking rather odd and old-fashioned perhaps – is exactly what you wrote, what the actors performed, years ago. Many dramatists of my generation despised this medium. They wanted nothing from film studios except cheques. I have been glad of the cheques too, but I never thought the screen inferior to the stage. Film has a different magic, that is all. And indeed, for many of the dramatic ideas I have had, it offered the better medium, being quicker to make its points, less literal and heavy with flesh, altogether more flexible, far better able to suggest change and the passing of time. It is not only closer to the novel than our picture-frame plays with their massive sets and all our contrivances for getting characters into and out of those sets, it is also closer in many respects to Shakespearean drama. True, the audience plays no part as it has to do in the Theatre : the performance is completed in advance and all the timing has to be guessed at; but on the other hand, if a film is well cast and skilfully directed, it stays well cast and skilfully directed, whereas plays can be murdered. Too often have I been invited, as a treat, to see plays of mine performed in distant places, and have then sat in torment. What is lost in one way is gained in another, and I would say that, considered as dramatic media, stage and film are roughly equal.

Why then did I write so many plays and so few films, no

really ambitious films? Why didn't *Time and the Conways* or *Johnson Over Jordan* or *Music at Night* arrive as films? Couldn't I have written them as films? Most certainly I could, and, if I had done, a lot of nasty little problems would have disappeared. Then why didn't I? Chiefly because I could write all three and get them on to the stage with less expenditure of time and energy than discussions and arguments with film producers, about a single one of them, would have cost me. And I detest discussions and arguments where my own work is concerned. I want to write and not sit in committee for weeks and weeks on end, especially if some members of it must have elephants or dancing girls in the next picture. I remember a film producer once saying to me: 'I don't know what's the matter with my writers. I give them good ideas, but they don't come up with anything worth doing.' I told him, rather sourly, that if he thought his ideas so good he should have turned them into film scripts himself. Many of my ideas have not been as good as I imagined they were, but good, bad, or indifferent, they have battered away at me, demanding to be expanded, shaped, given verbal substance, and if I had found myself condemned to go creeping around in the slow-motion world of film production, I would probably have gone out of my mind. I am not now simply asserting that the conditions of film production were bad, though they certainly were for an independent-minded writer when I knew them. I am also saying that I was temperamentally unfitted to challenge and overcome those conditions. I lacked both the patience and the tenacity.

The man – he is usually a director, not primarily a writer – who can compel the film industry to serve his purpose will probably have few ideas but uncommon tenacity. He has to hold a dream in an iron grasp. He must carry his idea, still fresh and untainted, through months, perhaps years, of discussions, arguments, challenges and ultimatums, as if he had sworn to bring a nosegay through ten cavalry charges and a peace conference. We may smile at the way in which Chaplin insists upon doing everything in his films – production and direction, story and dialogue, music and all. But it is not only his comic genius that has given us the Chaplin films, it is also his determination, defying all obstacles, to do what he wanted to do, to go his way and nobody else's, purpose and will providing the opportunities for the comic genius. I have often wondered how much original and sensitive work has been lost to films, not because the men capable of doing such work did not exist but because they shrank from or were defeated in the campaigns to keep films unoriginal and insensitive. And it is no coincidence that the best films have generally come from countries at times when film production has been financially shaky, threatened with bankruptcy: Germany and Russia in the Twenties, France in the Thirties, Italy just after the war. At these times the money-lenders are not in control, and films are made by men who simply want to make films. And here I must find space for my belief that, both in films and the Theatre, for every pound that has been lost over-estimating public taste at least a hundred pounds have been thrown away in timidly and tediously imitating previous successes.

When in the Thirties I spent two winters in the Arizona desert, with nine of us to keep there, I could motor in a day to Hollywood and there pick up some odds and ends of script work I could do back on the ranch, taking the magic money away before it turned into dead leaves. An inspection of credit titles in the middle and later Thirties will not reveal my name, for I surprised and gratified my script-writing colleagues by demanding to be left out of the credits. I never worked under contract in Hollywood itself, refusing many offers to do so, but I have paid it many visits. The first time I was there, over thirty years ago, it was hardly out of its mythological age. Astonishing characters, larger and wilder than life, walked in and out of imitation Spanish castles. At parties the men arrived unshaven, wearing sports shirts, while the women were in full evening dress, glittering with precious stones. The place was daft but not boring. Now all that look of a golden boom-town has gone. Hollywood seems to belong to worried business men wrestling with tax problems. Everybody appears to be sensible, even if rather too optimistic about the old brandy and Post-Impressionist art offered for sale on the West Coast, and rather dull. Down the years I have met more Hollywood stars than I can begin to recollect. As everybody – and even the most superior persons are not above this weakness – wants to know what they are like, these legendary beings, I must reply that they are like the rest of us, except that a few are genuinely great performers, and almost all are more photogenic than we are. My happiest hours in Hollywood were spent playing tennis. The best evenings were those in which Charlie Chaplin and Groucho Marx had some part. I have no romances with exquisite celluloid princesses to report: I held on to my drink and listened to talk about films, agents, Louis B. Mayer, diet, astrology, diet, Louis B. Mayer, agents, films, always hoping I would think of something witty and memorable to say and be given a chance of saying it.

Though never seeing myself as a film man, it is with film men, ready to fill days and nights with vain discussion, and not with publishers and theatre managers, that I have wasted most time on projects that came to nothing. I have written films of various sizes and kinds, but they must be outnumbered by the films I never did write in the end, after all the talk had subsided. The subjects ranged from the steel industry to Beethoven's Ninth Symphony. No money ever changed hands: only the hours were spent. But sometimes handsome cheques came to me out of the dream factory, without any film ever being made. What happened to prevent their being made I have never understood, the dark enigmas of film finance and production being beyond my comprehension. Over a quarter of a century ago, I was paid five thousand pounds, a fine sum in those days, for a film story, a good one too, about a famous international string quartet, four middle-aged bachelors of different nationalities. The producer who acquired it never filmed the story; he sold it for seven or eight thousand pounds to another producer, a Central European, who, as far as I know, never did make a single film in this country. Where that script is now, I don't know and can't imagine. No doubt those four string-players are now years out of date, but I still remember them with regret.

Just after the war, the Dutch writer, Jan de Hartog, was one of my neighbours in the Isle of Wight, and we amused ourselves concocting a fantastic film story that we called *Tober and the Tulpa*. For some years it was always about to be made, that film, by somebody or other. After that, every six months or so, I would find myself having lunch with or giving drinks to a new visitor from the studios, crazy, he would announce, about doing *Tober and the Tulpa*. I hesitate to say even now that the script has at last been forgotten, for, if I do say so, the next post will bring me an invitation to discuss it, probably, as so often before, from some stranger. I am not pretending ignorance, like some judge building up his importance, when I add that I have never been able to understand this world of film production. It is a mystery to me how scripts vanish and then turn up again, who all the people are, exactly when and how final decisions are made, where the money comes from and where it goes to, or what most men in that world think they are doing. What I do know is that I am temperamentally unfitted for dealing with it, so that much as I admire the medium itself, often wistfully considering its possibilities, I have never thought of turning myself into a full-time film man. Conditions may be better now; but I am worse, and prefer a quiet life.

8

There may run through these reminiscences – I hope not, but wouldn't bet on it – an undercurrent of feeling, a ground bass of grumbling, suggesting I have not been sufficiently praised. I will now confound the opposition by announcing that one of my activities was ridiculously over-praised, so much so that I dislike hearing it even mentioned. I refer to my wartime broadcasting, or at least to those broadcasts I made for listeners at home. This qualification is necessary because my chief task on the air, which I had to undertake on top of a lot of other work, was broadcasting several times a week, always very late at night, to America, the Dominions, and in fact, through recordings transmitted every hour or so, to all parts of the world where English was understood. These were longer than my home talks; there were of course far more of them; and the conditions in which they were written and delivered, especially during the Blitz periods, were not always easy. Letters by the hundred arrived from overseas to tell me how enthusiastically these talks were being received, particularly in Canada and Australia. Later, when I visited these Dominions, all traces of this enthusiasm appeared to have vanished with victory.

Nevertheless, it was an extra broadcast to Canada, which I undertook with much grumbling, that probably saved my life. This was in September 1940. I had just moved into the Langham Hotel, to be close to Broadcasting House and the late-night job. I had done two broadcasts on the Sunday, and would be up late again on Tuesday, so, being free on Monday night, I decided to go to bed early for the sleep I badly needed. But then a message came from across the road, begging me to do an extra broadcast on the Blitz specially for Canada. Growling and cursing, I agreed to do it, and left the Langham for Broadcasting House while the going was still good. I never returned to the Langham. That was the night when bombs fell all round Broadcasting House. The room in which I had planned to enjoy an early night was in that part of the hotel which was sliced off by a bomb. Probably that early night would have lasted for ever. Two days later I ran into Edward Hulton, who invited me to spend my first free night in the shelter bedroom he had had constructed below the basement of his house in Mayfair. The prospect was delightful – at last I could get out of my clothes (I said at the time that I had always looked as if I slept in my clothes and that now I actually did), and huddle luxuriously between clean sheets. This I prepared to do, slowly and with satisfaction, disregarding the remote sounds from the mad world above. But it was a night of incendiaries. I was just about to enjoy those clean sheets when I had to jump into my clothes again. The house was on fire.

The bright eyes of danger have never fascinated me. If I am not quite a coward, I am much closer to being one than I am to being any sort of hero. Yet I can honestly declare that on the whole I enjoyed that time, those splintered nights, those mornings when the air was the freshest ever tasted. Even later, during the buzz-bomb time, when I appeared to be fire-watching every night in Albany, where I lived, and had to make do with about two hours' sleep, so that afterwards exhaustion struck me down and I was hurried into an operating theatre, I liked living in a West End that suddenly seemed to be empty. We were all an improvement on our unendangered selves. No longer suspicious of gaiety, we almost sparkled. What more than half the English fear and detest is not threatened disaster, material insecurity, sacrifice or danger, but boredom. They should be offered crises, not guarantees of prosperity and security. There is of course among us, too widely reflected in our legislation, a minority of life-haters, enemies of everything sensuous and generous, adventurous and creative. In 1940–41, for once, the rest of us escaped from their influence, felt free, companionable, even – except while waiting for the explosions – light-hearted. It took bombs to deliver us. The old-fashioned kind, of course, not the improved sort we have heard so much about, coming out of an appalling life-denial (and notice how many embittered exiles have worked on them), and only capable of delivering us – and the very trees and grass – from existence itself. Meanwhile, politicians who appear on television might be reminded that this is the same nation that fought the war, that it might be worth risking some appeal to generosity of mind and heart, a feeling for dramatic high endeavour, imagination rising above self-interest. Every time I turn them on, they smirk at me as if they were selling washing machines and detergents.

All that is by the way. Now I return to those home broadcasts, those Sunday night 'Postscripts' that were so ridiculously over-praised. They took about ten minutes to deliver, usually between half an hour and an hour to write. They were nothing more than spoken essays, designed to have a very broad and classless appeal. I meant what I said in them of course: a man is a fool if he tries to cheat the microphone. (Add television cameras, and an artful experienced performer can risk some insincerity.) No doubt I had the right voice and manner, but then so had plenty of other men. I didn't see then – and I don't see now – what all the fuss was about. To this day middle-aged or elderly men shake my hand and tell me what a ten-minute talk about ducks on a pond or a pie in a shop window meant to them, as if I had given them *King Lear* or the *Eroica*. I found myself tied, like a man to a gigantic balloon, to one of those bogus reputations that only the mass media know how to inflate. I never asked for it, didn't want it. This sudden tremendous popularity, which vanished in a few years and indeed was put into reverse by the same mass media, gave me no pleasure, merely made me feel a mountebank. Voices cannot be disguised, and if I went into a crowded shop or bar all the people not only had to talk to me but also always had to touch me – I had thousands of hands laid on me – as if to prove to themselves I was more than a disembodied voice. There are people who open out like flowers in such an atmosphere, gracefully and smilingly accepting all popular tributes. I have never pretended to be one of them.

The first time I stopped these Sunday night talks, it was at my own request, for I felt I had had my share of this peak hour and other men ought to be given a chance. When I was brought back, after much clamour, I added some minutes and more edge to the talks. This time I was taken off the air. This annoyed me, not because I was anxious to continue these home broadcasts – I was still busy with the overseas talks – but because I dislike being pushed around, especially when I can't discover who is doing the pushing. I received two letters – I kept them for years but may have lost them now – and one was from the Ministry of Information, telling me that the B.B.C. was responsible for the decision to take me off the air, and the other was from the B.B.C., saying that a directive had come from the Ministry of Information to end my broadcasts. While blaming each other, I think both of them were concealing the essential fact – that the order to shut me up had come from elsewhere. I don't know how other people feel about this stealthy hocus-pocus, but to my mind it is one of the most contemptible features of British public life. Power is exercised in such a way – a nod here, a wink there – that it can't be challenged. We are democratic and free in theory but not in practice. Work may be censored as it is elsewhere, but not openly, through a censor's office everybody knows about; it is quietly shuffled and conjured away. Men are squeezed out of public jobs, not for political reasons – oh dear no! – but because they are discovered to be not quite the right type, not sound, old boy. This is the British way, slimy with self-deception and cant, and the older I get the more I dislike it.

With the Ministry of Information I was never on cordial terms. As a writer who made too much noise and didn't seem to know his place, I was regarded with suspicion. There were plenty of writers, innocently anxious to serve their country, working there in Malet Street. Not one of them was given a position of any importance and authority: lawyers, advertising and newspaper men came first. When Duff Cooper, whom I liked as a man, was Minister, we had a few sharp differences of opinion. For example, when I agreed to broadcast about the men of the Merchant Marine, I felt we had no right to praise them in wartime without assuring them that we would improve their working and living conditions in peacetime. To thank a man publicly, tears in your eyes and voice, while conveniently forgetting that his fo'castle was a hell-hole and his wife and children lived in a slum, seemed to me a job for Pecksniff. I know, because they told me, that a lot of people were fighting the war to keep Britain exactly as it had been – not possible, anyhow – but none of them had lived in back-to-back houses mostly on tea, bread and margarine. When Brendan Bracken was Minister of Information, he asked me to go and see him. He put a hand on my shoulder and said I was a wonderful writer and broadcaster but that I ought to keep off politics and social criticism, I ought to be like Dickens. Of all writers – Dickens! (Shaw once said that reading *Little Dorrit* had made a revolutionary out of him.) And this from a Minister of Information! Telling writers what to do!

My relations with the B.B.C. were pleasant enough, though I never felt that its senior administrators, men who wanted a quiet life and an hour or two in the garden, were on my side. To them I looked – and perhaps still look – like trouble. Following me would be nasty comments in the press, questions in the House, angry telephone calls from retired admirals. So a legend grew that as a broadcaster I was 'difficult' – 'better not risk him, my dear fellow' – and this was entirely false, for if I undertook to give a thirteen-minute talk, that is what I gave, and I was punctual and reasonably clean and sober. I have arrived in provincial studios and been made to feel I was a bomb with a trembling detonator. When I left, the sigh of relief followed me down the street. If I was ever surly or aggressively sharp with the people I had to work with in any of the studios, then I apologise here and now. I might have been a bit ungracious with one or two director-generals, but that is because top types don't bring out the best in me. The Establishment manner immediately acts as an irritant.

After sampling and performing on radio and television in many countries, I still think the B.B.C., with all its faults, the best network in the world. Though several old friends are now in charge of commercial television, both as a writer and a viewer I prefer the B.B.C. But I wish it were not so over-planned, so heavily responsible, so portentous, behaving as if it thought the Coronation was still on. When I am there, hoping for a quick whisky before it is time to perform, I always feel that Richard Dimbleby is in the next room, wearing his special face for the arrival of royalty and the Archbishop of Canterbury. So brightness falls from the air. There is an easy

informality, a suggestion that radio and television might be
fun, when one is working with the Canadian and Australian
broadcasting companies that is missing here in Merrie
England. I have agreed to do something and then have gone
and done it, in New York, Boston, Toronto, Ottawa, Mel-
bourne, Adelaide and several European cities, in less time and
with less fuss than it takes to exchange preliminary letters
with the B.B.C.

Television here suffers from a false importance. This was
inflated by the solemn chumps who ring up to say what they
like and don't like, by the popular dailies, and by all those
members of Parliament half-crazy for time on the air. Outside
light entertainment, where rewarding reputations can be
made, it is nothing like as important as programme con-
trollers and producers imagine it to be. One enquiry has
already proved that its political influence has been enormously
exaggerated. It can make reputations very quickly, but they
are not solid reputations, they are easy-come easy-go. One
reason why poor Gilbert Harding was so unhappy was that he
knew he was perched on a vast rotten mushroom. The sheer
quantity of attention that television receives is of course
formidable, but the quality of that attention is dubious. If it
were sharper and more demanding, half the stuff – particularly
all those empty interviews – would never be tolerated. Most of
us, enjoying a smoke after dinner, are content to stare at
programmes we would never leave the house and go fifty
yards to see. We watch and listen in an idle dream, passing the
time digestion takes. No urgency is communicated. We could
smile or yawn at scenes of torture and murder. Very little
appearing on that tiny screen in the living-room seems quite
real, even less of it excitingly significant. There may be something we all watch until our eyes ache – I for one drop all work
when Test Matches are being televised – but out of pro-

grammes designed to pass everybody's time painlessly we cannot expect to find much that will be either urgent or delightful. Really good television, I believe, will begin when we have to pay something, on the night, to see it. We shall give it a different kind of attention, and demand value for money.

We have no duty, whatever some people may think, to make appearances on television. Every invitation to do so must be considered on its merits. If I have steadily refused to contribute a word or a look to programmes like *This is Your Life*, that is because I think they are sentimental claptrap. If I declined to appear on various programmes to talk about *Literature and Western Man*, that is because I said all I wanted to say in the book itself. I didn't want to make publicity appearances on its behalf any more than I want to sit in a bookshop autographing copies. I have been face to face with John Freeman on many pleasant occasions, but I saw no reason why we should dish up our acquaintance to follow Sunday evening's cold mutton and salad. (Moreover, I don't like my face.) I am neither against television nor for it, simply as a medium, but I do resent being invited to talk about anything and everything so long as I do not feel strongly about it. I will, for example, gladly explain why I believe the nuclear deterrent to be essentially immoral, unworthy of any civilised power, and so much imbecility as Britain's chief defence, but that is precisely what I am not asked to do.

On the other hand, if I were starting to write now I think I would concentrate on TV drama, even though it is still poorly paid. I would master the technique, ready for the time when there would be a wider choice of programmes, possibly some pay-to-look drama. This could be subtle and fascinating, the most intimate drama the world has known. A writer of talent could have a wonderful time with it. The special scaled-down acting, which doesn't need theatrical 'projection', is already here. I notice a lot of young TV players who are admirable. Indeed, at present the acting is far better than the writing. This may not be the fault of the writers, who may be compelled to deliver what are in effect scripts for tiny-budget films or bungalow problem pieces – Why won't Dick ask Kate to marry him? – Has Sid lost his job? – What's worrying Mum and Dad? The TV drama I have in mind would not try to compete with films – no crowd scenes, airliners crashing, chariot races, big effects. It would bring viewers close to a few characters, whose relationships would be explored to the last flicker of an eyelid. It might at times be completely subjective, showing how a certain situation appeared to this one, that one, the other one. It would be adult, thoroughly civilised, and probably ruinous. Even so, I think that if I were even twenty years younger I would be experimenting with this new drama of people in close-up, of talk overheard and not thrown at an audience, of gestures and looks caught in quick glimpses, turning viewers for fifty minutes into recording angels. As I write this, I begin to feel the old stirring, I long to break off and put a few ideas into a notebook, to attempt creation in another form and place, committing myself all over again.

This brings me, not without some resistance, to that other 'commitment' we have read and heard so much about during the last few years. Should writers be 'committed'? Have I been 'committed'? If not, ought I to have been? Well, if 'commitment' means that a writer follows a party line, becomes a mouthpiece for a group of politicians, I have been as uncommitted as the west wind. Indeed, I have always thought that politicians should follow writers, not writers politicians. Who have more time for reflection? Who know more about human nature? Who can be disinterested because they are outside the struggle for place and power? Let the politicians practise the 'art of the possible' in Westminster, but let them also refresh their minds, give their souls an airing, well away from those benches and committee rooms, listening to writers among others. They won't of course, partly because they no longer have the time, partly because they are too conceited. (We are conceited too: the difference is that we *know* we are.) One reason why most of us no longer understand where we are is that politicians now control so much of our life, they have no time to think about it. We have evolved a very strange kind of democracy in which a few men never escape from politics while the rest of us, wondering what next, helplessly stand about, gaping, powerless. I have actually been told, more than once, in public rebukes, that if I choose to sit at home instead of in the House of Commons, I should mind my own business and not write about political affairs. But I live here, don't I? On the day I am allowed to live here free of all tax, smoking tobacco on which no duty has been paid, I will take notice of such rebukes, and not before.

I have never been a member of any political party. Some people, including two members of the present Government, have publicly denied this, in effect calling me a liar. But I know who has done the lying. It is true that before the 1945 Election I spoke at scores of meetings on behalf of Labour candidates. It is also true that a few years later I did a Labour Party political broadcast, on the understanding that Labour, if returned, would call a great national conference of the arts. All I did get was the works from the other side. I reached a depth of unpopularity as ridiculous as the giddy heights of popularity had been ten years before, in 1940. (I was still the same man.) My natural sympathies move to the Left; I am a pink, and a pleasant healthy colour it is too. Nothing could be sillier than the idea that there is some professional cunning in this. The people whom I was ready to champion, from the early Thirties onwards, do not buy novels and theatre seats and would not care if all the writers in England dropped dead. I lost one set of patrons, with money to spend, without gaining another. Moreover, the more important representatives of the Left didn't like me; sometimes I think they don't like anybody. It is the Right and the Establishment that look after their own.

In a reasonably tranquil world I could be happy writing away without giving a thought to political and economic life. It is against such a clear unchanging background that novels and plays are best written. At such times it is easier to look closely at men and women, to describe, in peace and quiet, the tragi-comedy of their antics. War, revolution, social upheaval in any form, they are all unfriendly to literature and the drama. In this age, which really belongs to journalists, if a creative writer opens his mind, the news comes screaming in, and his work suffers. If he tries to close his mind, to hoard his sympathy, his work still suffers. If he refuses to show indignation, to sit on platforms, to sign appeals, he is considered a self-centred ivory-tower type. If he doesn't refuse, then he is soon thought to be a show-off crackpot, one of the starry-eyed do-gooders. You can't win.

Whenever I have been goaded into writing an aggressive political piece, letters have poured in saying that I was quite right – but what was I going to *do* about it? The people who send such letters cannot understand that to an author writing is doing, that when he has written he has taken action. Beyond the printed page is another world that most writers – and I am certainly one of them – enter without confidence and probably with loathing. It is a world of meetings, from intrigues in a smoke-room corner to committees talking on and on long after the last oxygen has gone, rising then from the Mechanics' Institute in Coketown (Ald. J. W. Smothers in the Chair) to the Albert Hall complete with Empire Loyalist imbecilities. Though I can make a public speech as well as the next man –

indeed, better than most: the trick is to avoid all those last thoughts, final conclusions, and to end quite unexpectedly – I regard the dubious little art of oratory with suspicion, considering it so much ego-swelling ham Theatre. I never stand on a platform, cadging applause, without feeling ashamed of myself. No sooner does a writer find himself in this world of meetings than he longs to escape, to be back at his desk, far away from chairmen's remarks and collections and votes of thanks. In the end he pleases nobody. The enthusiasts in the cause see him as a half-hearted shifty prima donna. Publishers and readers are sure he cannot be the writer he was. Press and public remember him when rebels are being condemned but forget him when, the cause having triumphed, men of goodwill, courage, and vision are being praised. He pleases nobody, least of all himself.

Away from that alien world, back at the desk where he belongs, a writer must decide for himself the range and depth of his commitment. He should not be compelled either to write or not to write about public affairs. I for one would have felt frustrated and angry if I could not have said anything about unemployment in the early Thirties, the Nazi menace from 1935 onwards, the hope of a better Britain emerging from the war, the mixture of wickedness and imbecility in nuclear defence. Living in another age, I might never have written a line about political concerns. Perhaps – for I can't be sure – even in this age I would have left them alone if I had been an artist first, last, all the time, instead of being, as I suspect, half an artist and half a damaged man of action. Perhaps, because of my background and upbringing, a twenty-first birthday lost in the Flanders mud, and diffidence and dubiety for ever lurking behind the bouncy self-confidence, I could not be entirely serious about anything except the well-being of our society itself. This is not how art and literature are created, but then

[229]

probably I was – as Wells candidly declared himself to be – a kind of journalist. Unlike some writers I could name, now glittering on full-dress occasions like Christmas trees, I had never planned a literary career, had never spent ten minutes wondering what the next upward move ought to be, who should be conciliated, who could be ignored. I didn't – as all the evidence proves – give a damn.

I wanted praise of course – we all do – and perhaps longed for it like those men who produce all kinds of clever tricks to excuse their appearance at a party. Now that I am nearer seventy than sixty and, though not at all a cosmopolitan type, always feel more important (which is what men of my age like to feel) outside England than I do at home, sometimes I wonder if I was unlucky in my birthplace. Further south I might now be called *maître* and, wearing a skullcap, receive homage every Thursday night and Sunday afternoon. Further north and east, clear-eyed solemn maidens might bring flowers to the house on my birthday. Unfortunately we have no sensible English equivalent of these signs of public esteem, except those pats on the head and shoulder from the Establishment, meant for better or worse men, not for me. But after all, it is only when the rain never stops and I feel jaded that I begin to wonder what and where I am; as soon as the sun comes out, I decide what to try next, the weight of forty professional years being lifted at once, so that I seem to be jauntily starting all over again.

Beginning these reminiscences, I promised irony. It runs through the whole story. I am essentially English, yet it is outside England I find most appreciation, though often meeting it with a glum stare, wondering what the hell to do with the huge laurel wreath weighing me down. I am too conventional for the *avant-garde*, too experimental for Aunt Edna; too extroverted for the introverts, too introverted for the out-

and-out extroverts; a lowbrow to highbrows, a highbrows to lowbrows. I succeeded with the essay form just when it was dying. I brought back the long novel, only to be almost outlawed in literary London because it pleased too many people. The play I wrote as an exercise, so badly received it was nearly withdrawn after a few performances, became one of the most popular plays of this century in the World Theatre. The film medium might have best suited my talent, but it was hedged round with the very conditions that defied and defeated my temperament. I was monstrously over-praised for ten-minute broadcast talks I could have done almost in my sleep. When later I wrote and spoke out of the clearest sense of duty, I was attacked as if I were a public enemy. The one big critical book I had always wanted to do I wrote years too late, turning critic when most readers didn't care if I turned greengrocer or barman. I am thought to be out-of-date by clever dull young men who, whether they know it or not, are grinding away at ideas I sketched some years ago in *Thoughts in the Wilderness*. The most lasting reputation I have is for an almost ferocious aggressiveness, when in fact I am amiable, indulgent, affectionate, shy and rather timid at heart. *Thou hast no enemy but thyself*. I know; and I have quoted it first.

However, the work – though not all of it, I hope – has been done; and it has gone out to many places, injured nobody, debased no civilised values, fleeted the hours for innumerable people, pinky-white, yellow, brown and black. For that writing, anyhow, unlike the people with all those good unwritten books and plays, I at least have had the time. The use I have made of it might have been better, it might have been worse.

Index